PRAISE FOR

Knowing the Shepherd

MW00575892

Sandra's Bible study draws the weary mother into Scripture to dive deep into the nature of God himself. It is simple and easy to use, but rich and full of truth, helpfully applied to the life of a mother. My heart was nourished and quickened with joy as this study invited me to gaze at the God of many names!

—**TILLY DILLEHAY,** author of *Seeing Green* and *Broken Bread*, co-host of *Home Fires* podcast

In *Knowing the Shepherd: A Names of God Bible Study for Moms*, Sandra Bretschneider tenderly guides mothers to the Lord by revealing glorious angles of who he is and by showing how God's character is the help moms need for the difficulties they experience. Throughout the study, Sandra teaches a helpful range of passages and genres in the Bible and the context in which they exist, so that women will come away better equipped to be led by God and his Word, confident that he truly is their Shepherd. This is an excellent and trustworthy resource for the overwhelmed mom who desires to seek the Lord in motherhood and needs a loving sister to guide her!

—**CAROLINE SAUNDERS,** author of *Better Than Life: How to Study the Bible and Like It*

Studying the names of God is a worthwhile endeavor for all Christians, but it is especially beneficial for mothers. God's names reveal his attributes, character, and nature; this knowledge equips us to reflect his image in our homes. In this powerful study, Sandra Bretschneider guides Christian mothers on a journey of discovery and renewal. Her heartfelt stories, thoughtful commentary, and piercing reflection questions will equip you to learn and apply the rich truth of Scripture to your life. I have partnered with Sandra on several writing projects in the past, and her insight into Scripture and ability to ask thought-provoking questions always encourages me. I highly recommend this book to anyone who is searching for intimacy with God and a purpose-filled existence.

—**SARAH KOONTZ,** Founder and Bible Study Author of Living by Design Ministries

We moms need all the encouragement we can get. But we may not realize our hearts seek the peace that's only available in God's Word. Through Sandra's gentle yet seasoned guidance, moms will learn how to study and meditate on God's names for both practical and spiritual help. In the trenches of motherhood, these names will serve as powerful anchors of hopeful truth. A convenient study ideal for moms who don't want to put their spiritual growth on the back burner any longer.

—**SARAH GERINGER,** author of *Transforming Your Thought Life* and
Transforming Your Thought Life for Teens

In a day when some books of motherhood are shallow and often don't help you spend time in Scripture, *Knowing the Shepherd* is different. Throughout this 4-week study, Sandra takes you through the biblical text and helps you to focus on the character of God as you study his names. This is a unique and helpful study for those desiring to see what God calls himself and how his character practically affects the high calling of motherhood.

—**JON MARK OLESKY,** Pastor of The Cross Church

Knowing the Shepherd

Knowing the Shepherd

———— A ————

Names of God Bible Study for Moms

Sandra Bretschneider

Sandra Brethschneider
KnowingTheShepherdBook@gmail.com

Scripture quotations are from the ESV® Bible (The Holy Bible, English Standard Version®), copyright © 2001 by Crossway, a publishing ministry of Good News Publishers. Used by permission. All rights reserved.

ISBN: 978-1-7376249-0-5

Publishing and Design Services: MelindaMartin.me
Editors: Rachel Adamus and Andrew Buss
Author Photo: Christin Szczesniak

To my three precious daughters:

Tahlia, Elyza, and Lydia.

CONTENTS

INTRODUCTION TO THIS STUDY

About a week after bringing my firstborn daughter home from the hospital, a good friend came by to drop off a meal. Her son was born a few months ahead of my daughter, so she was well acquainted with the struggles most new moms face. I won't forget the moment I pulled her aside in my sleep-deprived state of mind and gushed, "I don't know what I'm doing! This is so hard!" It was an awkward moment, to say the least, but despite my embarrassing outcry, my friend patiently responded and stayed a while longer to listen.

I share this story to help paint a picture of my struggles as a new mom. Undoubtedly, motherhood was not an easy transition for me. I continued to struggle after that conversation with my friend, but what made it most challenging was the fact that I consistently neglected time with the Lord. Before I became a mom, I cherished copious amounts of quiet times with the Lord early in the morning with a hot cup of coffee in hand. Then I had my baby girl, and everything changed drastically. If I couldn't pursue God in a perfectly quiet house with no distractions, I simply didn't pursue him at all. My concept of time with him was figuratively placed within the confines of a box. Inevitably, after my daughter was born, I rarely spent time with him.

For months, I journeyed through a spiritual desert until the Lord led me out of it. Shortly before my daughter turned one, I finally grasped the importance of seeking God beyond the confines of a formulated box. I learned to seek him in the quiet and in the chaos, in the morning and throughout the day. Even though the challenges of motherhood remained, my hope was renewed in the Lord as I began consistently abiding in him. Instead of turning to temporary comforts when life got hard, I sought the Lord in prayer more often. When parenting challenges came, I prayed for wisdom rather than frantically reading as many books or articles as I could.

Even though those earlier days of motherhood were difficult, I believe God used them for good and, ultimately, to lead me to him—my Shepherd.

I'm now a mom to three young daughters who are nine years old and under. Life is very different for me with older children, but I continue to struggle in similar ways from when I was a new mom. Raising children is physically, mentally, and emotionally draining, and in more ways than one, I'm always in need of help. Rather than turning to God first, my natural tendency is to look elsewhere for comfort or guidance. Unfortunately, social media, search engines, shopping, time with friends, and good books always leave me wanting or searching for more. In these moments I have to continually remind myself that the Lord is who my soul longs for. He is my Shepherd who will fill the longings of my soul, comfort me in my distress, strengthen me in my weariness, and guide me with wisdom. He is the one I need to seek after first.

Over the next few weeks, my hope is that you too would be continually led to our Shepherd, our all-sufficient God who promises to gently lead us.

Isaiah 40:11 tells us, "He will tend his flock like a shepherd; he will gather the lambs in his arms; he will carry them in his bosom, and gently lead those that are with young."

No matter what stage of motherhood you may be in right now, I pray that your understanding of the significance of this verse will grow in the weeks to come. Together we will journey through Scripture and develop our understanding of who God is.

I'm ecstatic to share more with you, but in the meantime, let me fill you in on how to approach this Bible study.

The aim of *Knowing the Shepherd* is for you to deepen your understanding of God's character and gain a renewed hope and trust in him. In this four-week Bible study, you will learn about twenty unique Hebrew names of God. This study will provide an overview of the characteristics associated with each name as they are revealed in Scripture, rather than providing an in-depth study of the names themselves.

The lessons include a short introduction, contextual information about the Bible passage,[1] and questions to help you engage with the text. Each day you will either study a passage in which the Hebrew name originated or study a passage in which the characteristics associated with the name are evident. Over the course of the study, you will also gain the necessary structure and direction to help you establish or maintain consistent Bible study habits.

You can approach this Bible study in two ways. One is for you to complete each lesson in a single sitting. Another is to break up the study components over the course of your day.

Whichever approach you decide, my prayer for you is simple: I pray that out of the riches of God's grace, you would grow in your understanding of who God is, be led into a time of refreshment, and overflow with hope and trust in him.

Friend, let's journey together and discover the incredible and multifaceted character of God—the one who promises to gently lead us.

How to Use
Group Discussion Questions

A t the end of each week, you'll find group discussion questions. If you choose to complete this study with a group, the questions will help you review the learned material from the previous week. For example, after completing week one during your personal study time, you'll then meet with your group to go over that week's discussion questions.

Most of the questions are taken straight from your personal study days. These questions serve as a guide to you and your group. I invite you to utilize all of these questions or just some of them. You're also welcome to come up with your own discussion questions related to the study.

But grow in the grace and knowledge of our Lord and Savior Jesus Christ. To him be the glory both now and to the day of eternity. Amen.

—2 Peter 3:18

Week 1

Yahweh Roi

"THE LORD IS MY SHEPHERD"

E very woman's journey of motherhood is unique. Even though we may differ in how we become mothers or in the challenges we face, I believe we can all be encouraged by the same promise in Scripture. Isaiah 40:11 says, "He will tend his flock like a shepherd; he will gather the lambs in his arms; he will carry them in his bosom, and gently lead those that are with young."

Over the next few weeks, we will journey through Scripture and discover the significance of this promise by learning more about God's character. Together we will study several of his Hebrew names as they are displayed in Scripture. As we develop our understanding of God's character, we will discover he is all-sufficient to lead us.

Before we begin, it's essential we understand that even though we will be studying one specific name and attribute of God at a time, God is one in essence. He is not made up of parts; rather, all his character is perfectly unified. No one attribute is more predominant than any other. All of who he is exists in perfect harmony.

My prayer for you over the course of this study is for the truths of God's character to sink deep within your soul so you may overflow with hope and trust in him.

Today we will begin our study by focusing on the Hebrew name of God, Yahweh Roi, which means "The LORD Is My Shepherd."

TODAY'S PASSAGE: ISAIAH 40:9–14

The book of Isaiah was written by Isaiah the prophet, and some scholars theorize that other unknown authors contributed to the book as well. Its main theme is God's plan of redemption for his people who have turned from him. Isaiah 40 was a prophetic message written to Judah, who later became exiled Jews living in Babylon.

INTRODUCTION

Imagine: God had just brought judgment on the people because of their continual disobedience. They were exiles living in Babylon, where they were forced to serve their captive nation that worshipped false gods and persecuted them for their faith (Daniel 1–3). Yet, during their time of exile, God commanded Isaiah to write words of comfort and hope to them (Isaiah 40:1). Let's take a closer look.

—EXAMINE THE PASSAGE—
WHO IS GOD AND *HOW* IS HE LEADING?

First, notice how many times the word *behold* appears in the passage. Clearly, God wanted the Jews to look to him during their time of exile. Remembering who God is would renew their hope. Knowing more of God's character affects our perspective of him. It certainly gives us a greater appreciation for him as our Shepherd. The same God who promises to *gently* lead us is also our *powerful* God who holds the waters in the hollow of his hand (Isaiah 40:12).

Slowly read over the passage and write down several attributes of God that are revealed in this passage. For example, Isaiah 40:13–14 reveals God is wise and omniscient.

For this next part, we're going to focus on all the verbs mentioned in Isaiah 40:11 in order to gain a better understanding of the unique ways God shepherds his flock.

First, go ahead and write down all the verbs that appear in this passage.

To gain a better understanding of the unique ways God shepherds his flock, we will uncover the original Hebrew words, the language in which the Old Testament was written, and gain a better grasp of the intended meaning. The verbs from Isaiah 40:11 come from the following Hebrew words:

- *Tend* comes from the Hebrew word *rā ʿâ*, which means "to pasture, tend, graze, feed"[2]
- *Gather* comes from the Hebrew word *qāḇaṣ*, which means "to gather, assemble"[3]
- *Carry* comes from the Hebrew word *nāśāʾ*, which means "to lift, bear up, carry, take"[4]
- *Lead* comes from the Hebrew word *nāhal*, which means "to lead, give rest, lead with care, guide to a watering place or station, cause to rest, bring to a station or place of rest, guide, refresh"[5]

Take a moment to consider the significance of each of these verbs and what they reveal about Yahweh Roi, our Shepherd.

In your own words, describe the unique ways God shepherds us.

How does your knowledge of God as your Shepherd impact your present circumstances as a mom?

Some moms may feel relieved to know God promises to lead them, while others may feel reluctant to follow his leading in all aspects of their life because of their desire for control.

Which category do you tend to fall into?

What does it practically look like for you to relinquish control and submit to God's leading in all areas of your life?

Now let's focus our attention on how God leads us to know his ways. Please read Psalm 25:4–5. In these verses, King David wrote about God's leading.

According to verse 5, how do we come to know and walk in the ways of the Lord?

If we look to God as our Shepherd, we must also follow his leading by abiding in his truth. The word *abide* simply means to remain in his truth, and one way to do that is by consistently spending time with him through Bible reading and prayer.

Think about the unique challenges of motherhood. What obstacles might keep you from spending consistent time with the Lord?

Setting aside time to be with the Lord is essential. Revisit the obstacles you wrote above. Now write down one goal you hope to accomplish over the next few weeks as you complete this study.

What practical steps can you take to meet your goal? For example, if you struggle with consistency, some practical steps could include setting your alarm clock for a specific time to wake up earlier or designating a portion of your day to complete your Bible study.

—YAHWEH ROI—

OUR SHEPHERD WHO LEADS US

Isaiah proclaimed a word of hope to the Israelites during a very difficult time of exile. During this time, he reminded them that God was still powerfully in control and would be the one to lead them forward. Though we are not faced with the same set of circumstances as the Israelites were, the same word of encouragement can be applied to us as God's chosen people.

No matter what motherhood challenges we are faced with, we can fully rely on Yahweh Roi. He is mighty in power, sovereign over all creation, wise beyond all measure, and our Shepherd who promises to gently lead us. Take a moment to reflect on the truths you learned today and offer a word of praise to God.

El Roi

"The God Who Sees Me"

Have you ever felt like your work went unnoticed? It's a terrible feeling, isn't it? As a new mom, I felt this way a lot of the time when my firstborn was an infant. On a typical day, my daughter would wake up, and I'd feed her, change her, play with her, and put her down for a nap. Then the cycle would repeat. While the rest of the world kept moving along, I repeated endless routines.

In a season when I felt hidden from most of the world, it was difficult to value the work I did as a mom. What I failed to realize about each day, including the mundane tasks that encompassed it, is that nothing is hidden from God.

Today we will focus on El Roi, which is the Hebrew name of God that means "The God Who Sees Me." When we feel our work goes unnoticed by the rest of the world, we can remember that God sees us. He is all-knowing, and nothing is hidden from his sight.

Today's Passage: Genesis 16

Genesis was written by Moses to the Israelites. Its main theme focuses on the family lineage that forms the nation of Israel. Prior to Genesis 16, God made a covenant with Abram (Genesis 15) in which the Lord promised to make a great nation out of his offspring.

INTRODUCTION

We're going to take a closer look at some of the characters mentioned in this story in order to gain a better understanding of the context in which God appeared to Hagar. The first character is Sarai. Based on Scripture, we can make several observations about her. Sarai was Abram's wife, and she was a beautiful woman (Genesis 12:11). She was also barren and attributed her barrenness to God's sovereignty (Genesis 16:2).

Let's make some observations about Hagar. Based on Genesis 16, what do we know about Hagar?

Hagar fled to the wilderness after Sarai treated her harshly. What does the mention of a wilderness tell us about the nature of Hagar's circumstances?

In what ways can motherhood feel like a wilderness at times?

—EXAMINE THE PASSAGE—
WHO IS GOD AND *HOW* IS HE LEADING?

Nothing is hidden from God's sight. In this passage, it's clear that God saw Hagar's dire circumstances, despite the fact she was only a slave. I can only imagine how desperately she needed his help. Consider your present circumstances as a mom.

What are some of your urgent needs right now?

God sees you right where you're at, just as he saw Hagar. In verse 8, God asked Hagar questions to which he already knew the answers.

Even though God sees everything, why is it good to share our needs, desires, and joys with him?

As sinful people, our natural tendency is not to turn to God first. Take a moment to consider why you may resist openly communicating to God about your day-to-day life.

What do you think it will take for you to pursue authentic communion with God throughout your day? If you feel as if you are intentional in pursuing time with the Lord throughout the day, describe how your time with him can be enriched.

God is the Alpha and the Omega, the beginning and the end (Revelation 22:13). Nothing across the expanse of time is hidden from him.

According to Genesis 16:10, what is God's promise to Hagar?

Scripture proves that God kept his promise to Hagar because she eventually became the mother of many people (Genesis 25:12–16). The fulfillment of God's promise to Hagar reveals El Roi is infinitely more than we could ever comprehend. Everything in every place *throughout all periods of time* is seen by him. Take a moment to reflect on the magnitude of this truth.

As a mom, what are some concerns you have about the future? For example, are you concerned about your child's academics or peer relationships?

Full reliance on God is commensurate with an absolute belief in his character. How does a deeper understanding of El Roi strengthen your trust in him to lead you?

Trusting in El Roi should positively impact our actions. Let's take a look at how Sarai and Hagar's actions differed in this passage. In verse 2, Sarai gave Hagar to Abram so an offspring would be produced. Sarai's actions proved she either did not believe El Roi or trust in him. If she did, she would have demonstrated her trust by waiting on God to provide an offspring through her and Abram. By way of contrast, Hagar revealed trust in El Roi after encountering him at the well. In verse 9, God told Hagar to return to where she came from. Take a look back at verses 15 and 16. These verses reveal Hagar's trust in El Roi because she returned to Abram as God commanded.

Consider all the daily work you do as a mom and how God sees everything. What are some of the tasks you complete each day that mostly go unnoticed by others?

How will the knowledge of El Roi change the way you approach your daily tasks?

Now let's be specific. Pinpoint a task and write down one practical way you will glorify the Lord as you complete it this week. For example, I can either begrudgingly wash the dishes or I can ask the Lord for strength to wash them with a thankful attitude.

—*EL ROI*—

OUR SHEPHERD WHO SEES US

When many of the everyday details of our lives go unnoticed by others, God sees us. What a comfort to know he is El Roi. He is the one who sees us when we're changing diapers, cleaning up spills, preparing meals, washing clothes, and driving our kids to school. May we lean into him each day by sharing our thoughts with him and walking in obedience, even when our actions and thoughts are hidden from everyone else in the world—except him.

Yahweh Tsuri

"The Lord Is My Rock"

When one of my daughters was two years old, she suddenly lost the ability to walk. In fact, within one night's sleep she woke up seemingly paralyzed from the waist down. Without hesitation, my husband and I took her to see a doctor.

The moments of waiting were agonizing. Questions of uncertainty bombarded our minds. *Did she contract a life-altering illness? Would it get worse? What would become of her?*

While fear of the unknown threatened to unravel us, we turned to the only one capable of stabilizing us—the Lord our Rock. Even though we didn't know what the future held, we knew our faithful God would be the one to bring us through it. And he did.

Thankfully, the doctor who treated her knew what was wrong. My daughter had contracted Toxic Synovitis. The prognosis was good because she would be able to walk again within a week or two. We felt extremely relieved to hear such an outcome!

In moments like these, when circumstances cause turmoil in our lives, we can turn to the Lord for help. God is Yahweh Tsuri, which means "The Lord Is My Rock." His character is enduring, faithful, and secure. Today, we will learn more of who he is as revealed in Scripture.

Today's Passage: 2 Samuel 22:1–7

The book of 2 Samuel, written by an unknown author, is a historical narrative recounting the reign of King David. Before 2 Samuel 22, David won a war against the Philistines. It was one of many victories the Lord granted to the Israelites.

INTRODUCTION

Yahweh Tsuri is referenced many times in Scripture. 2 Samuel 22:1–7 is only one of many references by King David. To better grasp the significance of the Hebrew name, it's helpful for us to understand the implication of a rock during biblical times. In ancient Israel, rocks were a symbol of strength, permanence, and security.[6] They were used to build walls and fortresses, and large boulders were used as a shield in times of battle.

According to verse 1, when was David's song of deliverance written?

King David was well acquainted with the battlefield. In your own words, briefly describe the nature of a battlefield.

—EXAMINE THE PASSAGE—
WHO IS GOD AND *HOW* IS HE LEADING?

In verse 3, David said the Lord was his Rock, in whom he took refuge. How is a place of refuge a provision of salvation during a battle?

There may be times in our lives when we feel like we're living on a battlefield (Ephesians 6:10–20). We are not fighting for our physical lives, but we may be faced with chaos, uncertainty, weakness, or temptation.

Reflect on a time in your life when you felt this way.

In what ways can the trials of motherhood feel like a battlefield?

Whenever we're in need, we can turn to the Lord our Rock. He is our firm foundation, faithful and unchanging. Name some practical ways we can turn to the Lord. For example, one way is by memorizing a verse we can recite whenever we are struggling.

Now let's turn our attention to another passage in Scripture. In Exodus 17, the Israelites were in the Wilderness of Sin and needed water. They complained to Moses about their thirst, and Moses turned to the Lord for help. Let's read in Exodus 17:5–6 how God provided for his people.

What did God tell Moses to do for water to come out of the rock?

Describe how the rock was life-giving to the Israelites.

The same rock from this passage in Exodus is mentioned in the New Testament. Let's look at 1 Corinthians 10:1–4 together. In these verses, the apostle Paul wrote to the church in Corinth about the Israelites.

According to verse 4, what did Paul write about the Rock?

The mention of Christ being the Rock who provided for the Israelites proves God's faithful presence with his people. How was the water from the Rock in Exodus 17:5–6 a means of salvation for God's people?

When we read Old Testament passages such as 2 Samuel 22:1–7 and Exodus 17:5–6, we must consider how the stories foreshadow Christ. Even though we may tend to view the Old Testament and New Testament as separate parts, they are all the same story of redemption, pointing us to the gospel of Christ as the Living Water for our lives.

Yahweh Tsuri, the Rock of *Salvation*, was a place of refuge and security for King David throughout numerous battles. God saved him from his enemies. Yahweh Tsuri was a stable provision of life-giving water for the Israelites during their time in the wilderness. God saved them from death.

Yahweh Tsuri provided salvation for us through the precious blood of Jesus. Our future is secure in him. Each day we must continue to look to him because he is our firm foundation.

How does our security of redemption in the Lord our Rock change the way we view and respond to the challenges of motherhood?

Abiding in God's Word each day is one way we can continually find strength and rest in the Lord our Rock. Think about a verse that you would like to keep at the forefront of your mind this week to help you continually abide in Yahweh Tsuri.

Write it out below or place it on a small notecard.

—*YAHWEH TSURI*—

OUR SHEPHERD WHO IS OUR ROCK

Whatever circumstances we face as moms, whether it's the uncertainty of our child's health, the chaos of child behavioral challenges, the difficulty in making parenting decisions, or the fluctuating emotions of our child's teenage years, we can turn to Yahweh Tsuri. He is our steadfast Shepherd who will faithfully lead us. Our hope is secure in him.

Yahweh Tsidqenu

"THE LORD OUR RIGHTEOUSNESS"

One day, while chatting with a group of other moms, I unintentionally became wrapped up in a discussion about education methods. I'd rather have discussed my weekend plans with these women, but instead I found myself attempting to formulate some well-thought-out explanation for why my husband and I decided on a private Christian school for our daughters.

Unlike the other moms, I didn't have a thoughtful response for some of the questions brought up. Inevitably, the more questions that were directed at me, the more I became defensive and second-guessed my decision.

The real problem was I wanted affirmation from the other moms. I needed to know I made the best choice for my daughters' education. I was convinced the success or failure of my decision determined whether I was a good or bad mom.

As moms, we make many choices for our kids each day, from which infant car seat to purchase to which first car we should give to our teen and everything in between. We all want to make the best choices, but none of the choices we make should define who we are. Only God can define who we are, and for those who are in Christ, we are made righteous through the blood of Jesus.

Today we will focus our study on Yahweh Tsidqenu, which means "The LORD Our Righteousness." As we develop our understanding of who he is, we will be encouraged to rest securely in him as we fulfill our roles as moms.

TODAY'S PASSAGE: JEREMIAH 23:1–6

Even though the authorship for the entire book of Jeremiah is uncertain, many scholars believe the prophet Jeremiah was indeed the author for the majority of the book. It contains many different literary genres, and the passage we will be reading is considered one of the prophetic passages. The purpose of the book was to communicate the chaos of the time period, to give a message to the people during that time, and to give a message regarding the future of God's people.

INTRODUCTION

In order to better grasp the significance of Yahweh Tsidqenu, we must first understand what righteousness is. Righteousness is characterized by morally right or just ways. Additionally, Isaiah 45:19 reveals that God defines what is right ("I the LORD speak the truth; I declare what is right"). Take a moment to let the truth of that verse sink in: God not only is righteous but declares *what* is right. He defines righteousness.

—EXAMINE THE PASSAGE—
WHO IS GOD AND *HOW* IS HE LEADING?

In Jeremiah 23:1, the shepherds God was referring to were the leaders of Judah. They were obviously not doing as the Lord commanded them to do because God's people, the sheep, were being destroyed and scattered.

Notice the word *therefore* in verse 2. The purpose of this word is to link verses 1 and 2. Let's determine the connection between these two.

According to verse 2, how will God execute justice? (Remember this is a prophetic passage, so it's communicating what is to come.)

Our righteous God must do something about injustice because it is wrong. If he overlooked the sin of his people, he would not be acting morally right. His righteousness would be null. Thankfully, we serve a righteous and just God, and we can trust his ways because they are perfect (Deuteronomy 32:4).

In God's righteousness, he not only informs the people how he will execute justice but also tells them what he will do to make things right again—that is, how he will properly shepherd his flock.

Slowly reread verses 3–6 and make a note of what the Lord plans for his people.

The coming of Jesus Christ is the fulfillment of verse 5. He is the metaphorical "Righteous Branch" prophesied for God's people. Let's now look up and read Romans 3:21–22, where the apostle Paul was writing to the church in Rome.

According to Romans 3:22, how do we receive the righteousness of God?

Knowing who God is and who we are in him should change the way we live each day, including the way we live out our calling as moms. Think of all the things you do and the choices you make as a mom.

Why is it sinful to want to do things perfectly, better than any other mom, and for the praise of others? (I invite you to look up 1 Corinthians 10:31 and 1 Peter 4:1–2 if you need help in answering this question.)

There's a difference between a mom wanting to do things perfectly for the praise of others and a mom who wants to do the best she can for the praise of God's glorious grace.

Describe the mom who lives for the glory of God.

Let's also spend a moment discussing the guilt we experience in failing to do things perfectly. Describe some of the mistakes you've made as a mom that have burdened you with guilt.

Describe the difference between guilt that leads to shame versus conviction that leads to repentance. Take a moment to confess any shame you've experienced as a result of not fully trusting in Christ as your righteousness.

God declares what is right, and he is the one who has declared you righteous through the blood of his precious Son.

How might resting securely in Yahweh Tsidqenu impact the way you react in failing to do things perfectly?

—*YAHWEH TSIDQENU*—
OUR RIGHTEOUS SHEPHERD

We have the righteousness of God through faith in Jesus Christ. We are mothers purified and sanctified for good works, not for our own glory but for the praise of his name. Take a moment and sit in awe of Yahweh Tsidqenu, our Righteous Shepherd, who has given you his righteousness through the work of Christ. Reflect on how the Holy Spirit may be leading you to repentance.

Yahweh Yireh

"The Lord Will Provide"

Around the age of three years old, one of my daughters suddenly began waking up multiple times during the night. Sometimes she'd wake up screaming and crying, refusing to be comforted. Other times she woke up for no reason at all. For a short while, I thought it was just a phase, but after several months it became the new normal. It was frustrating because even after attempting multiple solutions, nothing worked.

Then, while praying with her one night, I finally came to a spiritual realization. I remember praying something like, "God, if this is what you have for us right now, then we will press on and keep seeking you." I decisively came to terms with the trial God allowed. From then on, I wasn't just praying for God to remove the hardship; I was relying on him to help me. I'd tuck my daughter in bed at night, expecting her to wake up and also trusting God to give me what I needed.

Whatever physical or emotional trial we experience as mothers, we can look to God to give us what we need. Today we will learn more about Yahweh Yireh, which is Hebrew for "The Lord Will Provide."

Today's Passage: Genesis 22:1–14

As you may recall from a previous day of study, Genesis is a historical narrative. Prior to Genesis 22, God made a covenant with Abraham and told him that he would be the father of a great nation (Genesis 12 and 15).

INTRODUCTION

To better understand the original intended meaning of this passage, we must unfold the text, verse by verse, and consider the whole context. As we move through the study together, think about what this passage reveals about God's character.

—EXAMINE THE PASSAGE—

WHO IS GOD AND *HOW* IS HE LEADING?

Let's begin by figuring out God's purpose in commanding Abraham to sacrifice his son.

According to verse 1, why did God tell him to sacrifice Isaac?

There's a difference between testing and tempting. Scripture is clear that God does not tempt us (James 1:13), but he does test the faith of his people (Exodus 15:25; 16:4). Consider the covenant that was made with Abraham. God promised that Abraham would be the father of a great nation, even though Abraham's wife, Sarah, was barren for many years. Finally, Sarah conceived and gave birth to Isaac, but then, many years later, God told Abraham to sacrifice him on an altar.

What was the significance for God telling Abraham to sacrifice his only son?

The type of sacrifice God wanted Abraham to offer was a burnt offering. The purpose of the burnt offering was to make atonement for sin (Leviticus 1). The sin and guilt offering were also offered for this purpose; however, the burnt offering was the most costly offering.[7]

Look closely at verse 8. Describe Abraham's faith in Yahweh Yireh.

After a dramatic sequence of events, we read how the Lord provided a sacrifice for the burnt offering. What did God provide for the sacrifice?

According to Genesis 22:14, the name of the mount where all of these events took place was called "The Lord Will Provide," which is translated from the Hebrew words *Yᵊhōvâ yir'ê*.[8] This is the place in Scripture where we obtain the name Yahweh Yireh because this is where God reveals himself as the one who provided.

God provided a burnt offering for Abraham, and atonement for sin was made through the offering of a ram. Hundreds of years later, God would provide atonement for his people through the death of his Son. Undoubtedly, this passage in Scripture foreshadows Christ's sacrifice for his people (Hebrews 10:10, 19–20).

Before we even begin to discuss how God provides for us each day, I want to emphasize our greatest need, which is salvation (Romans 3:23; 6:23). God is holy, and we are sinful people. Without salvation through Jesus Christ, we face the wrath of God (John 3:36). Thankfully, God provided atonement for our sins through Jesus' death on the cross.

Take a moment to ponder the magnitude of this truth: God gave his Son for us. Whenever we doubt God's provision, even for a moment, we must remember the truth of the gospel. God granted us salvation through the blood of his precious Son. He provided a means for us to know him and have life in him. Because God provided a means for salvation—our greatest need—we can trust that he will provide for us each day.

Briefly describe the many ways God has already richly provided for you.

Reflect on some of the needs you have right now, including the ones related to parenting your child(ren).

In what ways do you need Yahweh Yireh to take care of you?

Who or what are you prone to trust to take care of your physical or emotional needs more than God?

Why do you think you sometimes turn to other things or people first before going to the Lord in prayer?

Please take a moment and summarize a gospel truth discussed during our study today that you will choose to recall when you doubt God's provision. I also encourage you to write it down on a notecard and place it where you will be reminded of it throughout the day.

When we ask God to provide what we need, we can expect him to give us all things in accordance with his will (Romans 8:32; 1 John 5:14–15).

Reflect on a time when God gave you what you needed in a way or timing you didn't ask him for. What was the outcome?

—*YAHWEH YIREH*—

OUR SHEPHERD WHO PROVIDES

Yahweh Yireh will grant us what we need in life, through every season of parenting. Even though our hearts may long for quick or easy solutions to our problems, we must trust God to give us what we truly need. Lest we ever lose faith in God's desire to take care of us, we must remember the cross. Truly, God is for us, and he will provide what we need in accordance with his good will.

WEEK 1
GROUP DISCUSSION QUESTIONS

INTRODUCTORY QUESTIONS

1.   What name of God resonated with you the most this week and why?

2.   What is something new you learned this week from your time of study?

DAY 1 — *YAHWEH ROI*: "THE LORD IS MY SHEPHERD"

1.   Read Isaiah 40:11. After studying the various verbs from Day 1, what did you conclude about God, our Shepherd?

2.   Read Psalm 25:4–5. Share what may keep you from spending time with the Lord on a consistent basis. What are some practical ways you can be intentional in spending time with the Lord during busy seasons of motherhood?

DAY 2 — *EL ROI*: "THE GOD WHO SEES ME"

1.   Read Genesis 16:7–13. In your own words, describe Hagar's dire circumstances. How can motherhood feel like we are navigating a wilderness at times?

2.   Share some future concerns you may have related to parenting. How does a knowledge of El Roi fuel your hope?

DAY 3 — *YAHWEH TSURI*: "THE LORD IS MY ROCK"

1.   Read 2 Samuel 22:1–7. Describe a time in your life as a parent when you depended on the Lord your Rock to get you through a difficult trial.

2.   How does your security of redemption in the Lord our Rock change the way you view and respond to the challenges of motherhood?

Day 4 — *Yahweh Tsidqenu*: "The Lord Our Righteousness"

1. Read Isaiah 45:18–19 and Romans 3:21–22. How do we receive the righteousness of God?

2. Discuss the guilt you may experience as a mom in failing to do things perfectly. What's the difference between guilt that leads to shame and conviction that leads to repentance?

Day 5 — *Yahweh Yireh*: "The Lord Will Provide"

1. Read Hebrews 10:19–23. Describe how God has already provided for us. How does this truth affect our trust in him to provide for our tomorrows—whatever they may hold?

2. Reflect on a time when God gave you what you needed in a way or timing that was different than what you expected. What was the outcome?

NOTES

Week 2

El Shadday

"God Almighty"

"Survival mode" is what my husband and I affectionately labeled the first few months of life with our firstborn. We had no idea how exhausting it would be to take care of an infant. For the first time, my husband began drinking coffee, while I, on the other hand, attempted to stay awake without it. The last thing I wanted was to prevent my breastfed daughter from taking a nap. In the early days, those glorious moments of quiet gave me an opportunity to recharge and were a token of God's grace. Inevitably, I anticipated nap times as much as a mini vacation.

Caring for our children can be exhausting! Thankfully, we can turn to the one who promises to strengthen us in our weariness.

Today we will learn more about El Shadday, which translates to "God Almighty." Even though there is debate as to the meaning of the name, there seems to be a central focus on God's power.[9] Undoubtedly, El Shadday is our all-powerful God who spoke the world into existence, offers life through Jesus, and promises strength to those who are weary.

Today's Passage: Job 37:1–13

The book of Job recounts the story of a man named Job who, as a faithful follower of God, suffered tremendously. Before chapter 37, Job and three of his friends passionately debated the reason for Job's suffering. Finally, in chapters 32–37, Elihu, a bystander to that point in this book, stepped in to direct everyone's attention to God and his character. If you read past chapter 37, God began to address Job directly.

INTRODUCTION

God's power is incredible! Aside from Job 37, countless other passages in Scripture point to his greatness. Let's recall a few of his works mentioned throughout the Bible:

- God spoke every living creature into existence.
- He brought a flood on the earth and protected his people.
- He parted the waters of the Red Sea.
- He fought powerful nations for the Israelites.

- He came to earth through a virgin.
- He bore his own wrath of judgment on the cross.
- He defeated death through his resurrection.

These are just a few of the works that display his power. Take a moment to recall a time in your life when God displayed his power. How does recalling God's past work in our lives renew our hope in him?

—EXAMINE THE PASSAGE—
WHO IS GOD AND *HOW* IS HE LEADING?

Let's continue our time of study by focusing on one aspect of El Shadday—his powerful voice.

Write a few brief descriptions of God's voice as revealed in this passage. For example, in verse 2, it's described as thunder.

What are some things God commands to happen on the earth?

In your own words, summarize what Job 37:1–13 is communicating about God.

It's one thing to read about God's power, and it's another for the truth of who he is to sink deep within our souls, resulting in praise and adoration.

Why do you think there is often a gap between head knowledge and heart realization?

El Shadday displays his power throughout all creation, and he is the one who promises to gently lead you. Take a moment to reflect on this truth and write some of your thoughts below.

What a privilege to be led by El Shadday. God's greatness is immeasurable and beyond our understanding. His power is limitless, and you know what else? El Shadday, whose voice thunders and roars with power, offers strength to his people.

Now let's read together in Isaiah 40:28–31. As you may recall, the prophet Isaiah was writing to the Israelites in this chapter.

What are the promises of verses 29 and 31?

The translation of the phrase "but they who wait" in Isaiah 40:31 comes from the Hebrew word *qāvâ*,[10] which means "to wait, look for, hope, expect."

In your own words, describe what it means to "wait for the Lord."

The two questions Isaiah 40:28–31 does not answer for us is *how* and *when* God will strengthen us; however, we can make some conclusions based on what other verses in Scripture reveal. We know from Isaiah 55:8–9 that God's ways are not like our ways. From 2 Peter 3:8 we discover that God's concept of time is not like ours. Therefore, God may renew our strength in ways we can't fathom and within a time frame that is different from our expectations.

Recall a time in your life when a moment of refreshment, strength, or rest was provided by God in a way or time different than you had expected.

Let's take what we've learned today and directly apply it to the challenges of motherhood. What tasks are depleting you of energy?

Name some practical ways you can rely on the Lord and his strength when you are weary from the daily tasks of motherhood.

—EL SHADDAY—

OUR ALMIGHTY SHEPHERD

By the power of El Shadday's voice, all creation submits to his authority and power. Nothing exists without him. The same voice that provides guidance to all of creation promises to gently lead you according to his perfectly timed plan. Take a moment to sit in awe of God's grace toward you.

DAY 2

El Simchath Gili

"God My Exceeding Joy"

When all three of my daughters were little, I remember looking forward to the day when they could do more on their own. Life seemed especially challenging when my oldest was four, my middle was two, and my youngest was a few months old. Every day seemed to go by in a flash and yet not quickly enough. It seemed like I rarely had time for myself.

Now that my daughters are older and more independent, there are days when I reminisce about their infant and toddler years. Even though I felt mostly sleep-deprived during those years, I miss them greatly.

What I learned from my experience is that when our joy is dependent on our circumstances, we will always fluctuate between contentment and discontentment. Our lives are constantly changing, and the unique circumstances we face as moms are ever-changing as well.

There will always be less-than-ideal circumstances that make parenting challenging. That's why our joy must not come from the temporal things of this earth, which are ever-shifting, but from the only one who is constant, faithful, and true.

Today we will focus our time of study on El Simchath Gili, which means "God My Exceeding Joy." As we journey through Scripture, we will discover that the Lord is the source of enduring joy, no matter what circumstances we experience in motherhood.

Today's Passage: Habakkuk 3:17–19

The prophetic book of Habakkuk was written to Judah. According to historians, it was written by the prophet Habakkuk before the Babylonian invasion of Judah. It is a short book in the Old Testament containing a discourse between Habakkuk and God.

At the beginning of the book, the author shares his complaints to God, and the Lord responds to him. By chapter 3, we can see a noticeable change in the author because his prayer to the Lord develops into praise. Habakkuk 3:17–19 is where we will be today. It is a small poetic passage tucked within the prophetic book.

INTRODUCTION

What a proclamation of praise! In fact, the last sentence in verse 19 indicates the author intended it to be a song of praise. Let's begin to unpack the different parts of this passage together.

First, look back at verse 17. What are some of the specific losses Habakkuk mentions in the verse?

Consider the period when this passage was written, many centuries before modern amenities. Summarize why these specific losses would amount to tremendous hardship for the people during that time.

Most of us can't relate to these types of agricultural loss, but we can relate to trials in general. Let's consider the types of losses or hardships that are unique to motherhood. Name a few that come to mind.

—EXAMINE THE PASSAGE—

WHO IS GOD AND *HOW* IS HE LEADING?

Remembering who God is in our passage helps us to understand Habakkuk's response.

Going back to verse 18, how does the author choose to respond to the Lord despite the possible circumstances?

It's easier for us to be joyful when our circumstances are ideal, like the times when we are able to sleep through the night without tending to a screaming child, our children are excelling at school, or we are able to find some time for ourselves. But what about the times when our children struggle through illnesses, other moms appear to have it more together than we do, or teenage drama nearly puts us over the edge? What about these days?

These days are certainly filled with loss and hardship. They give us plenty of reason to linger in the mud of discontentment, so let's turn back to Scripture to learn where our joy must come from. Look closely at verses 18–19.

Why can Habakkuk rejoice in the Lord?

We can be joyful in every circumstance because God is the source of our joy! Let's continue our understanding of El Simchath Gili by studying Isaiah 44:21–23. If you recall from a previous day of study, Isaiah was written to Judah who was later exiled to Babylon.

According to this passage, what are some of the things the Lord did for his people?

According to verse 23, what should be the creation's response to the Lord's redemptive work?

Now take a moment to reflect on all the Lord has done through your story of redemption. Write your thoughts below.

Salvation through Jesus gives us a reason to always rejoice, no matter our circumstances, but what might it look like for us to apply this truth to our life as we live out our calling as moms? First, let's develop our awareness of any areas of discontentment. Think about your role as a mom, the unique stage of parenting you are in, the trials your children are going through, your work situation, and the support you have.

What are you unhappy with? When do you find yourself complaining the most?

When we are unhappy with the way things are, we can choose to set our thoughts on the God of our salvation. We can remind ourselves of all the Lord has done for us in sending Jesus Christ to redeem us from our life of sin.

What are some other ways you can rejoice in the Lord when you are struggling with discontentment?

For this last part, let's create our own song of praise to the Lord by utilizing the literary structure from Habakkuk 3:17–19a. Fill in the spaces below with your own words.

When _____

and _____.

Even if _____

or _____.

Yet I will _____.

—EL SIMCHATH GILI—
OUR SHEPHERD WHO IS OUR JOY

Our joy will not last when it is dependent on our circumstances. El Simchath Gili is the only source of lasting joy. So when we are picking up toys for the millionth time during the day, we can choose to rejoice in the God of our salvation. When we are struggling to make sense of our adolescent's poor life decisions, we can rejoice in Jesus' death and resurrection. No matter what circumstances lie ahead of us in this ever-changing journey of motherhood, we think of El Simchath Gili. In him we always have a reason to rejoice.

Machseh

"Refuge"

I'll never forget the day my husband and I brought our daughter home from the hospital. The ride was long, and all I could think about was my baby girl strapped in her car seat. *I hope she's okay. I wonder if the strap is too tight. Is she still breathing?*

While my husband drove, I incessantly checked the rear mirror. "She's just sleeping," he reassured me, "It's going to be okay. We're almost home."

As it turned out, my husband was right. My daughter was fine, and eventually we arrived home safely.

Looking back on that time in my life, I realized I worried way too much as a new mom. Aside from my daughter's car seat straps, I worried about nap schedules, feeding options, crib safety, minor colds, and the list went on and on!

As moms, we will always have concerns about our child's well-being. Today it may be our child's health issues, and tomorrow it may be our child's peer influences. Whatever our concerns may be, we can turn to the Lord for help.

Today we will learn more about God our Refuge. The Hebrew name is Machseh, which means "Refuge." As we develop our understanding of who God is, we will be encouraged to rest in him.

Today's Passage: Psalm 46

The book of Psalms is a compilation of poetry and contains a lot of figurative language. The purpose for each of the psalms was to lead the Israelites to worship. King David was the main author of the majority of the psalms; however, other authors also contributed to its compilation.

Psalm 46 is in the category of a song of confidence. Its purpose was to strengthen the Israelites' trust in the Lord.

INTRODUCTION

What can be more terrifying than watching the mountains fall into the heart of the sea? I can't imagine! Yet God doesn't want us to fear. He tells us that he is our refuge in times of trouble.

Let's take a moment and focus on the word *refuge*. A place of refuge simply means a place of security from distress or danger.

Given this definition, why would a mom find comfort knowing God is her refuge?

Notice the word *therefore* in verse 2. This word is a connective word. It's connecting verse 1 with verses 2 and 3.

What is the connection between these verses?

Verses 2 and 3 also contain exaggerations. However, the writer was making a point with these exaggerations: we shouldn't fear anything because God is our refuge, strength, and help.

Name some examples of common things moms worry or fear about.

What are you most anxious or fearful about right now? Pause for a moment and share these burdens with the Lord. Ask him to reveal any underlying sin, and spend some time confessing it to him.

—EXAMINE THE PASSAGE—

WHO IS GOD AND *HOW* IS HE LEADING?

In Scripture, words or phrases are emphasized with repetition. Look back at this passage and write down or make a mental note of how many times the phrase "with us" is mentioned. God our Refuge promises to be with us and to provide the shelter we need in times of danger or distress.

Are you absolutely convinced of this truth? Please explain.

Verse 10a says, "Be still." Now, visualize a place of refuge in a war zone. Without a place of refuge, a soldier would be scrambling to protect himself from the enemy. A place of refuge would be the only place a soldier could be still. Likewise, we can be still when God is our refuge.

What might it practically look like for you to be still in times of distress?

We're going to briefly jump to the New Testament and look at Matthew 14:22–33. In this passage, Jesus had just fed five thousand people and told his disciples to get in a boat and meet him on the other side while he dismissed the crowds. Later, as his disciples were in the boat, Jesus began walking toward them on the water. Let's read about Peter's response in Matthew 14:22–33.

At what point did Peter become fearful?

Keeping our eyes on God our Refuge is the only way we can experience peace in moments of worry or distress. Isaiah 26:3 says, "You keep him in perfect peace whose mind is stayed on you, because he trusts in you." What a wonderful promise.

As we end our study, I want to invite you to practically apply some of the truths we've discussed today.

First, briefly revisit some of the worries or fears you wrote down earlier in today's lesson. Then, write down several characteristics of God in the space below.

Now go through the characteristics of God you listed above, and this time underline each one of them. As you underline each characteristic, pause to praise God for who he is. It can go something like this: "God, you are powerful. You are loving. Thank you that you have full power over this situation in my life. I praise you for your unconditional love." As you praise him, allow the truths to sink in. My hope is that this simple exercise will help you fix your eyes on him—our Machseh.

—*MACHSEH*—
OUR SHEPHERD WHO IS OUR REFUGE

Regardless of what stage of motherhood we are in, our worries can burden us to the point of heightened anxiety. Thankfully, we can turn to God in times of distress. He is our Machseh and strength, an ever-present help in trouble. We have no need to fear.

DAY 4

Elohim Kedoshim

"The Holy God"

During a typical week, my days are filled with many different tasks, from meal preparations and laundry to homework and bedtime routines with my kids. Even though my daughters are old enough to do many things on their own, they are still dependent on me much of the time.

Some days I'm tempted to think part of the work I do as a mom is insignificant, but this is far from the truth. Each day I'm caring for the physical and emotional needs of my children. When I nurture them in light of the gospel, I'm also living in holiness and glorifying God. The daily tasks I do for my children *are* significant.

As Christian mothers, we are called to a life of holiness because we serve a holy God. This means we must live differently from the world and look to God, who sets the standard for living.

Today we will learn more about Elohim Kedoshim, which means "The Holy God" in Hebrew. As we reflect more deeply on God's character, we will develop our understanding of how he calls us to live holy lives for him.

TODAY'S PASSAGE: LEVITICUS 20:22–27

Leviticus was written by Moses and is a type of utopian literature, which contains information about how people are supposed to live, including any explanation for specific practices they may have. Leviticus specifically contains laws and regulations for how the Israelites were commanded to live as an established nation in the land of Canaan.

INTRODUCTION

When we read a passage in Leviticus, we must remember this is a book written for the purpose of communicating how the Israelites are to live as God's chosen people, holy and set apart for his glory. Although we are no longer under these rules and regulations as recipients of salvation through Jesus, we should not turn a deaf ear to God's living and active Word. Through careful study of Leviticus, we can grow in our knowledge and adoration of who God is and gain a greater appreciation for Jesus' work of salvation.

To begin our study, let's formulate an overview of Leviticus 20:22–27. Slowly reread the passage and summarize some of the main points it communicates.

—EXAMINE THE PASSAGE—
WHO IS GOD AND *HOW* IS HE LEADING?

Now let's take a moment to develop our understanding of God's holiness. In *Systematic Theology*, Wayne Grudem writes, "God's holiness means that he is separated from sin and devoted to seeking his own honor."[11] Undoubtedly, every action of God is holy.

List ways in the passage that God reveals his holy character (i.e., he abhors those who are unholy [v. 23]).

According to verse 26, why is God commanding the Israelites to be holy?

Acting out of his own holiness, God commands the Israelites to live holy lives in Leviticus 20:22–27. Today we will pinpoint only a few of the regulations instituted by God that shepherd his people unto holiness.

From today's passage, name some ways in which the Israelites were called to live.

Verse 27 reveals the capital punishment for those who were mediums or into witchcraft. This was one of many instances in which capital punishment was commanded (Leviticus 20:2, 9, 10). When we read about severe consequences for sin, we must remember God's holiness. Everything he says or does is holy.

What do his actions against sin disclose about his character and the mark we need to meet if we want to draw near to him?

Just as God calls the Israelites to live holy lives, separate from the other inhabitants of the earth, he calls us to live the same. We will now turn our attention to 1 Peter 1:14–19. In this passage, the apostle Peter was writing to Christian exiles in Pontus, Galatia, Cappadocia, Asia, and Bithynia.

According to this passage, summarize how we are to live.

Think about how a typical, non-Christian mother might go about daily tasks, conformed to worldly standards. Now consider the life of a Christian mother. Give some examples of how she can live a God-honoring life as she takes care of her children.

Look back at verses 18 and 19. Why is it essential for us to keep the gospel at the forefront of our minds as we strive to live holy lives?

Reflect on the tasks you do for your children each day. In what ways is the Holy Spirit convicting you to live a holy life as you go about your motherly duties?

Lest we forget, Elohim Kedoshim is our standard for holiness, and he is the one who empowers us to live holy lives by his Spirit (2 Corinthians 3:18; Galatians 5:22–23). As we abide in him each day, he will transform us so we may be fruitful for his glory (John 15:4–5).

Describe the difference between living a self-empowered "holy" life and living a Spirit-empowered holy life.

As we near the end of our time of study for today, let's ponder all that we've learned about Elohim Kedoshim and how he promises to lead us "in paths of righteousness for his name's sake" (Psalm 23:3b).

How does the truth about his character affect your trust in his leading (Isaiah 40:11)?

—ELOHIM KEDOSHIM—
OUR HOLY SHEPHERD

Knowing God as Elohim Kedoshim should deepen our desire to live holy lives. When we're confronted with sin, we should pursue repentance. Instead of seeing our children's needs as interruptions in our day, we should tend to them with a joyful attitude—not necessarily because the tasks are easy, but because we are redeemed and sanctified to love our children for God's glory. Elohim Kedoshim is the one who directs our steps to live holy lives, and by his Spirit he will conform us into the likeness of his Son.

Take a minute and read Revelation 4. Then close your eyes and reflect on the holiness of God.

El Kanna

"The Jealous God"

If I'm honest, a quick scroll through my phone can turn into something more. Especially when I choose to jump on social media and scroll through post after post of nearly perfect pictures of moms with their kids. As I thumb through the feed, I wonder how the other moms look so put together chronicling another fun day of activities. And how their family's outfits always seem to coordinate with their home decor.

Despite my perplexity, the temptation to compare my life to theirs is often too great. If I linger a bit more, the ideologies they represent become my devotion.

The problem is, God is the only one worthy of devotion. He is holy, worthy of praise, and jealous of his own glory. Today we will learn more about his jealousy as we study the Hebrew name El Kanna, which translates to "The Jealous God."

Before we begin, I invite you to pray and ask God to give you a greater understanding of his character as we study this attribute that is frequently misunderstood by many.

Today's Passage: Joshua 24:14–28

The book of Joshua is a historical narrative, and the author of the book is uncertain. One of the purposes of the book is to emphasize God's faithfulness to the Israelites as they begin to settle into the land of Canaan. In Joshua 24:14–28, Joshua is speaking to the Israelites about renewing their covenant with the Lord.

INTRODUCTION

What comes to mind when you think of the word *jealous*? Undeniably, the word brings up many personal connotations that most likely don't provide a thorough understanding of it.

There are two different meanings for the word. One has to do with the jealousy of another person. In this connotation, jealousy is sin because the root of it is our desire for our own glory. Our desire to be the best is a means to magnify ourselves. However, we don't deserve any glory or honor because we're not God. Attempting to exalt ourselves and receive the glory that is not due to us is sinning against God, who alone is holy and worthy of praise.

Another meaning for the word *jealous* has to do with zeal. When we study about the jealousy of God, we must think of his character within this connotation. God is a jealous God, which means he is zealous for his own honor and glory. And unlike us, God's honor and glory *is* rightfully his because he is holy. In *Systematic Theology*, Wayne Grudem writes, "God's jealousy means that God continually seeks to protect his own honor."[12]

In what ways does this definition clarify any misunderstanding you may have had about this attribute of God?

—EXAMINE THE PASSAGE—
WHO IS GOD AND *HOW* IS HE LEADING?

Take a look back at Joshua 24:14. The word *fear* in verse 14 comes from the Hebrew word *yārē'*, which means "to fear, revere, be afraid."[13] Based on the context of verse 14, the word *fear* is indicating reverence.

Now that you have a better understanding of this word, summarize verse 14 in your own words. How is God calling the Israelites to live?

Remember God's holiness. He alone deserves the honor. What's the problem with the Israelites worshipping other gods?

God shepherds us to know him as El Kanna so we can rightly assess whether we are walking in his ways in our everyday lives. We may not have statues in our house that we bow down to each day, but we are still prone to idolize other things, whether they are material things or ideals of living. Let's try and pinpoint some idols unique to motherhood.

What are moms prone to worship other than God? Try and think through the different ages and stages of motherhood as well.

Ideals are standards of perfection. How do ideals for living become idols in our lives (e.g., our desire to feed our children certain foods, place them on the perfect sports team, or educate them with the best methodology)?

How many times did the Israelites tell Joshua they would serve the Lord in this passage?

At first glance, we may wonder why Joshua said in verse 19 that the Israelites would not be able to serve the Lord, but we must read the verse in context to understand why. First, in verse 19, Joshua asserted that the Israelites' commitment to serve the Lord should not be done casually. Additionally, we discover a very important piece of information that will help us understand why Joshua said what he did in verse 19. In verse 23, Joshua told the Israelites to put away their foreign gods.

Describe how the Israelites' worship of foreign gods contradicted their desire to serve the Lord.

Even after the Lord delivered the Israelites on multiple occasions (Joshua 24:1–13), they continued to worship other gods. Like the Israelites, it's easy for us to say we will serve the Lord and commit ourselves to holy living, but it's harder to actually follow through in obedience.

El Kanna alone deserves all the honor and praise because he is holy.

How do the idols in our life take away from our devotion to the Lord? Try to be specific with your response.

One way we can be intentional about living for God is by repenting of any idols in our lives and asking the Lord to change us. Pinpoint some of the idols in your life specifically related to your unique role as a mother. Spend some time repenting of these things in prayer.

What is one step of obedience you can take to turn away from these idols?

God seeks to protect his own honor, which is more proof of his holiness. He alone is deserving of devotion. No other thing or person is worthy. If he condoned worship of unholy things or people, he would not be holy. The fact that he is a jealous God and condemns idolatry is more proof of his holiness.

Today we studied a frequently misunderstood attribute of God. How will your new insight from today's study affect your life moving forward?

—EL KANNA—

OUR JEALOUS SHEPHERD

El Kanna is glorious! There is no other thing or person worthy of worship. His ways are pure and just, and he alone deserves the praise. What a reassurance to know our God will shepherd us in paths of righteousness for his name's sake.

WEEK 2
GROUP DISCUSSION QUESTIONS

INTRODUCTORY QUESTIONS

1. What name of God resonated with you the most this week and why?

2. What is something new you learned this week from your time of study?

DAY 1 — *EL SHADDAY*: "GOD ALMIGHTY"

1. Read Job 37:1–13. What does this passage reveal about God's character?

2. Read Isaiah 40:28–31. What are some practical ways you can rely on God and his strength when you are weary from the daily tasks of motherhood?

DAY 2 — *EL SIMCHATH GILI*: "GOD MY EXCEEDING JOY"

1. Read Habakkuk 3:17–19. What might it practically look like for us to rejoice in the Lord, no matter the circumstances we face as moms?

2. Share your personal song of praise to the Lord that you filled out at the end of this day's study.

DAY 3 — *MACHSEH*: "REFUGE"

1. Read Psalm 46. What are some common things moms worry or fear about, and what might it practically look like for you to seek God for refuge?

2. Read Isaiah 26:3. Share some of the characteristics of God you wrote down at the end of this day's study. Recall a time in your life when God displayed these characteristics in your life.

DAY 4 — *ELOHIM KEDOSHIM*: "THE HOLY GOD"

1.   Read Leviticus 20:22–27. What does this passage teach us about God's holiness?

2.   Read 1 Peter 1:14–19. Describe the difference between living a self-empowered "holy" life and living a Spirit-empowered holy life.

DAY 5 — *EL KANNA*: "THE JEALOUS GOD"

1.   Read Joshua 24:14–28. Describe what it means that God is a jealous God. Feel free to look back to the introduction of Day 5.

2.   What are moms prone to worship other than God? Try and think through the different ages and stages of motherhood. How do the idols in our life take away from our devotion to the Lord?

NOTES

Week 3

DAY 1

Shophet

"Judge"

When it comes to raising our children, the choices we make are significant. As we learned earlier in our study, we are called to a life of holiness, which should impact how we raise our children. Intentional parenting is challenging though. Each day we're bombarded by messages from worldly standards. Sometimes it's simply easier to let go of some things out of pure convenience. For example, I can attest to the ease of not following through with discipline at a moment when one of my kids interrupts me. At other times, it's easier to let my kids go about their day in the morning rather than initiating a short morning devotional beforehand.

However, the Bible is clear about how we should parent. We are called to train our children in the discipline and instruction of the Lord. One day we will have to give an account for how we live, including the choices we make in raising our children (Deuteronomy 6:7; 2 Corinthians 5:10).

Today we will develop our understanding of God as our Judge. The Hebrew name is Shophet which means "Judge." As we grow in the knowledge of who God is, we will be encouraged to grow in a manner that is pleasing to him.

TODAY'S PASSAGE: PSALM 94:1–15

As you may recall, the book of Psalms is a compilation of poetry, so it must be read as poetry. Psalm 94 in particular is a psalm of lament. It was a song for the Israelite community to sing when they were oppressed by the wicked.

INTRODUCTION

God is a righteous judge. In holiness, he determines who is unjust and pronounces vengeance on those deserving of his wrath. God's judgment on evil is proof of his holiness.

Describe some of the prevalent evil mentioned in Psalm 94:2–7.

Unlike the evildoers, how are God's people blessed according to Psalm 94:12–15?

—EXAMINE THE PASSAGE—
WHO IS GOD AND *HOW* IS HE LEADING?

What is Psalm 94:9–11 ultimately communicating about God?

We are dependent on our righteous God to deliver justice against evil. Psalm 94 is a psalm of lament, but it ends with a hope fully set on the Lord.

What does Psalm 94:22–23 reveal about God our Judge?

God knows everything, including the motives of our heart (Proverbs 21:2). How should this truth positively impact the way we live?

As we consider how we should live in light of God our Judge, we will now turn our attention to 2 Corinthians, where the apostle Paul wrote to the church in Corinth. Please read 2 Corinthians 5:9–10.

When the apostle Paul mentions "home," he is referring to being in the presence of the Lord. Undoubtedly, Paul has a desire to please the Lord with his life while on earth.

What does verse 10 reveal about our future?

One day we will stand before God, who will judge all our actions while here on earth. Take a minute to allow the weight of that truth to sink in.

Consider all the fruit of the Spirit—love, joy, peace, patience, kindness, goodness, faithfulness, gentleness, and self-control (Galatians 5:22–23).

As you consider your natural tendencies in how you care for your children and the temptations you face as a mom, which one specific area do you see the need to grow in during this season of your life?

What is one action step you can take this week to set yourself up for success to walk by the Spirit (Galatians 5:16)?

Deuteronomy 6:7 commands us to raise our children in the ways of the Lord. Describe how you would like to live in greater obedience to this command. Try to be specific with your response by including a plan of how you will be more intentional.

—*SHOPHET*—

OUR SHEPHERD WHO IS OUR JUDGE

God our Shophet leads us in paths of righteousness, and we must make hard choices each day to follow him. A life of holiness involves a life of sacrifice, but it's all done for the glory of God. When we choose to patiently care for our children for the millionth time during the day, God sees it. When we exhibit self-control in a moment of dispute with our kids, God knows it. When we choose to faithfully pass down the Word of truth to our kids, God hears it. God is our righteous Judge, the one who determines our steps, and we must faithfully follow him.

Elohim

"God, Mighty Creator"

About nine weeks into my first pregnancy, my husband and I saw our oldest daughter for the first time on an ultrasound screen. It was a memorable moment, one I'm sure I'll never forget. Our baby girl was about one inch in size and already had a steady heartbeat. Even her tiny arms and legs were beginning to take shape. We were in awe!

Seeing our daughter on the ultrasound screen that day was like having a front-row seat to God's workmanship.

Undeniably, God is a magnificent Creator. There is no other who speaks life into existence. He is Elohim, which means "God, Mighty Creator." Today we will learn more of who he is and gain a greater understanding of the purposes he designed for us.

Today's Passage: Genesis 1:26–31

Genesis contains the historical narrative for the origin of creation, sin, and the Israelites. Prior to today's passage, God spent the first five days creating the entire universe, except for the land animals, man, and woman. Then, on day six, he created the land animals and Adam and Eve.

INTRODUCTION

Before God began creating the heavens and the earth, Genesis 1:2 tells us, "The earth was without form and void, and darkness was over the face of the deep. And the Spirit of God was hovering over the face of the waters." God then created the heavens and the earth.

—EXAMINE THE PASSAGE—
WHO IS GOD AND *HOW* IS HE LEADING?

Out of the void, God brings forth beauty. He meticulously designs everything into existence and brings order to it all.

What do his ways reveal about his character? List some adjectives that come to mind.

In verse 26, circle the word *us*. Some scholars believe this is the first hint of the Trinity—God the Father, God the Son, and God the Holy Spirit.[14] Further proof of this conclusion is found in Colossians 1:16a and Job 33:4. When the apostle Paul wrote about the preeminence of Christ in Colossians 1:16a, he said, "For by him all things were created, in heaven and on earth." Also, in speaking about the Spirit, Job 33:4 says, "The Spirit of God has made me, and the breath of the Almighty gives me life." These verses reveal both the Son and Spirit were also at work in creation.

Another interesting truth from the creation account is that man and woman are the only ones who were *formed* by God (Genesis 2:7, 21–22). Everything else he spoke into existence.

What does this truth reveal about who God is and his relationship with us?

According to Genesis 1:27, what is unique about us?

What a privilege to be made in the image of God! It's a truth we may never fully grasp until we are in eternity with him! Through the work of his Spirit, we can reflect his glory by showing love, joy, peace, patience, kindness, goodness, faithfulness, gentleness, and self-control.

As image bearers of God, we can also create and put things in order. Think about the simple tasks of creating meals for your family or bringing order to clutter or uncleanliness in your home.

How can these mundane tasks be a means of worshipping God (1 Corinthians 10:31; Colossians 3:23)?

Elohim gave purpose to all of his creation. In Genesis 1:29, we discover how he created plants and trees with seed so we could eat of their fruit and propagate more food.

Take a moment to read through the passage again and write down some of the purposes God designed for the man and woman.

To "be fruitful and multiply" is a twofold command given by God. First, we are called to be fruitful. Let's focus on the ways we can be fruitful in motherhood.

What might fruit-bearing look like in the context of Christian motherhood?

Second, the command is to multiply, which includes both physical and spiritual reproduction. Spiritual reproduction is the faithful stewardship of the gospel to unbelievers, immature believers, and younger generations. Put simply, God calls us to multiply worshippers for him (Matthew 28:19–20; Revelation 7:9–10).

We are now going to look closely at a short passage in Deuteronomy. In this passage, Moses was communicating the Lord's commandments to the Israelites. Please read Deuteronomy 6:6–9.

The Israelites were responsible for passing down their faith to their children by teaching them all that the Lord commanded of them. We are commanded to do the same as present-day Christians.

Notice the word *diligently* in verse 7. This adjective tells us how we are to teach our children, and the word comes from the Hebrew word *šānan*. In this context, the Hebrew word means "to sharpen, teach (incisively)."[15] To teach incisively means to be clear and direct in our teaching.

Name some practical ways moms can diligently teach their children the ways of the Lord.

In what ways are you discipling your children, and in what ways would you like to grow in this area?

Adam and Eve were given the command to be fruitful and multiply before the fall (Genesis 3). But as a result of their sin, they didn't fulfill this command perfectly, and neither do we. Romans 3:23 reminds us that we all fall short of the glory of God. Thankfully, for those who are in Christ, we have a new life and are empowered to live for him (Romans 6:23; 2 Corinthians 5:17).

What are some specific reasons you are tempted to become complacent in the area of discipleship?

How can you be more intentional in fulfilling one of God's purposes in your life to "be fruitful and multiply"?

—*ELOHIM*—

OUR SHEPHERD WHO IS OUR CREATOR

Out of the void, Elohim created life and designed order. All of his creation submits to him, is sustained by him, and is purposed to serve him. Nurturing our children is just one of the many ways we can glorify God. He designed us to nurture life, and he will equip us with what we need to be fruitful and multiply followers for him.

Yahweh Tsebaoth

"The Lord of Hosts"

When one of my daughters had trouble sleeping one night, I shared the sweet promises of Psalm 46 with her. She was afraid of the dark, and I knew the psalm would bring great comfort to her.

Psalm 46:7 and 46:11 both say, "The Lord of hosts is with us; the God of Jacob is our fortress."

While my daughter lay wide awake in bed, I explained the significance of what it meant that the Lord of hosts is with us. I said something like, "God is the commander of armies and armies of angels. He has power over everything. And you know what? He promises to be with you."

I won't forget the look in her eyes when I shared that truth with her. Her brown eyes lit up in amazement; her change in demeanor made me smile. Shortly afterward, she finally fell asleep, comforted by the Lord's promise.

Today we will learn more about Yahweh Tsebaoth, which means "The Lord of Hosts." His name means that he is the ruler of all the physical and spiritual realm, and he is our powerful God who also promises to gently lead us.

Today's Passage: 2 Kings 6:8–17

The book of 2 Kings is a historical narrative written by an unknown author. Much of the monarchy of ancient Israel is recounted in the book. A well-known prophet, Elisha, is one of the main characters in chapter 6.

INTRODUCTION

The king of Syria was warring against Israel, but in the end, they did not prevail. In fact, later on in Scripture, 2 Kings 6:23b reveals that "the Syrians did not come again on raids into the land of Israel."

Let's take the time to carefully unfold the context of this passage. First, according to verse 12, who was the "man of God" referenced in verse 9?

How did the king of Syria respond when he discovered Elisha was the one who revealed the king's plans to the Israelites?

According to verses 14 and 15, describe the extent of the Syrian army.

What was Elisha's immediate response when his servant came to tell him about the Syrians?

—EXAMINE THE PASSAGE—
WHO IS GOD AND *HOW* IS HE LEADING?

Yahweh Tsebaoth was with the Israelites. Elisha had the spiritual eyesight to see the myriads of angelic armies that were surrounding them. He had no reason to fear because his confidence was steadfast in the Lord.

Describe the greater magnitude of the Lord's angelic army according to verse 17.

Like Elisha's servant, we too may become fearful or overwhelmed by our circumstances. And just like the servant, we need spiritual insight to grow our confidence in the Lord of hosts, who is with us and for us. The Lord shepherded Elisha's servant into seeing the spiritual reality by opening his eyes. Let's consider where we need God's shepherding in light of who Yahweh Tsebaoth is.

What aspects of motherhood overwhelm you to the point of anxiety or dread?

Who or what do you tend to rely on most to get you past these feelings?

What are some spiritual benefits when we turn to God first?

Let's now turn our attention to Deuteronomy, where Moses informs the Israelites of how they are to put their confidence in the Lord during times of warfare. Please read Deuteronomy 20:1–4.

Look back at this passage and pay special attention to all the statements that reveal God is with the Israelites and for them. List some of the statements below.

We may never experience a physical battle, but Scripture tells us that there are many spiritual battles we will face while on earth. Ephesians 6:12 says, "For we do not wrestle against flesh and blood, but against the rulers, against the authorities, against the cosmic powers over this present darkness, against the spiritual forces of evil in the heavenly places."

Consider how motherhood sometimes brings out the worst in us, often exposing sin we were previously good at hiding. What are some areas of sin you are struggling with?

How can an awareness of the spiritual forces that are up against you change the way you battle temptation?

The Lord of hosts is with you, and he wants you to have victory over sin in your life. How does the knowledge of who God is, Yahweh Tsebaoth, increase your confidence and hope to battle sin?

Describe some practical ways you can use what you have learned about Yahweh Tsebaoth to strive to honor him.

—YAHWEH TSEBAOTH—
OUR SHEPHERD WHO IS THE LORD OF HOSTS

Yahweh Tsebaoth is the ruler of all the physical and spiritual realm. Everything exists by him and for him (Colossians 1:16). Even though we can't see the extent of his dominion and rule, we must have the faith to believe it. When motherhood overwhelms us to the point of despair, whether in the circumstances we face or the temptations we battle, we must look to him. Surely Yahweh Tsebaoth is with us and for us. Our confidence resides in him.

DAY 4

El Emunah

"The Faithful God"

Several baby books, written by experienced authors, guided my first few months as a mom. One day, after reading one of my books, I distinctly remember formulating a schedule for my firstborn onto notebook paper. When the schedule didn't go as planned, I quickly re-read parts of the book while cradling my daughter in my arms. My approach was ridiculous, but I was in desperate need of guidance.

Now I realize that no matter how experienced the authors were, none of them could guarantee their methods or words of advice. I learned the hard way with my firstborn.

Thankfully, God's Word and character are different. We can fully rely on him and his promises because he is El Emunah, "The Faithful God." Throughout Scripture, God's Word proves his faithfulness. As present-day Christians, we have the privilege of leafing through pages of Scripture (which equate to hundreds of years) to see God's faithfulness displayed time and again.

Today we will learn more about his faithfulness as we focus on a time in history when the Israelites were slaves in Egypt.

TODAY'S PASSAGE: EXODUS 6:1–8

Exodus was written by Moses to recount the Israelites' deliverance from Egypt. Prior to Exodus 6, the Lord appeared to Moses in a burning bush (Exodus 3) and told him that Moses would lead his people out of Egyptian slavery. In Exodus 5, Moses approached Pharaoh for the first time and asked him to release the Israelites; however, instead of letting them go, Pharaoh increased the Israelites' workload.

INTRODUCTION

Through an unfathomable chain of events, God delivered the Israelites. One of the most beautiful things about the exodus story is that it foreshadowed the deliverance of God's people, both Jews and Gentiles, through the death and resurrection of Jesus. Today, we will take a closer look at what this particular passage reveals about God's faithful character. The first thing we need to do is identify the covenant promise from this passage.

According to verse 4, what is the covenant promise?

—EXAMINE THE PASSAGE—
WHO IS GOD AND *HOW* IS HE LEADING?

Hundreds of years passed from the time that God established the covenant with Abraham (Genesis 15) until the time of Moses. After the exodus, the Israelites waited many more years before they inhabited Canaan. Throughout the hundreds of years from when the covenant was made to the realization of the promise, a lot of hardship and suffering occurred. Take a moment to let these facts sink in.

What does this truth reveal about God's faithfulness and timing?

How will this knowledge change the way you face periods of waiting?

Let's focus on a phrase that is repeated a few times throughout the passage. Notice the phrase "I am the LORD" every time it appears in the passage. This phrase is significant because it emphasizes the fact that God would be the one to deliver his people.

How many times is the phrase mentioned in this passage?

When God made a covenant with Abraham hundreds of years prior to Moses, not many specifics were provided as to how God would fulfill his covenant (Genesis 15). Now we read about some of the specifics of God's plan in this passage. Let's identify some of the details. Fill in the blanks from information found in Exodus 6:6–8:

- (v. 6) I will _____ you out from under the burdens.

- (v. 6) I will _____ you from slavery.

- (v. 6) I will _____ you with an outstretched arm.

- (v. 7) I will _____ you to be my people.

- (v. 7) I will _____ your God.

- (v. 8) I will _____ you into the land.

If we were to continue reading in Scripture, all the way up through Joshua, we'd read more specific details about how God fulfilled his promise (i.e., Joshua 1:2; 3:12–13; 6:3–5; 24:1–13). Think about the time period of Abraham, Moses, and Joshua and the extent of details that were revealed to each of them as God fulfilled the covenant.

What can we conclude about God's faithfulness?

Let's apply what we've learned today to the challenges of motherhood. What are you prayerfully waiting for?

There are many different things moms may be tempted to rely on more than God. Daily schedules, financial blessings, and extra sleep are just a few of them.

What other things or people could moms be tempted to rely on more than God?

Throughout the expanse of biblical history, beginning with the promise of the Messiah in Genesis 3:15 to the fulfillment of Jesus' death and resurrection, God remained faithful. There is absolutely no question about his character. We can rely on him and his Word (Proverbs 30:5).

As you consider the challenges you are facing today, what's a promise in Scripture you will cling to? Write it down below.

Discouragement is inevitable. We all face it, but what's most important is what we do when we are faced with discouragement. Think about what we've learned about El Emunah, our faithful God.

What specific truths will you choose to remember when faced with discouragement? Write these truths down below.

—EL EMUNAH—
OUR FAITHFUL SHEPHERD

El Emunah's Word proves his faithfulness. We can fully rely on him. No matter what challenges lie ahead, whether it's the laundry piled up in our laundry room, academic problems for our kids, or peer relationships among our children, we can lean into God's character and trust him to lead us through. El Emunah will not fail us. Take a moment to reflect on his faithfulness. Ask him to develop your trust in him

DAY 5

Elohim Chaseddi

"God of Mercy"

Sometimes when I lie in bed at night, the weight of the day lingers in my mind. Inevitably, feelings of regret often come up. Whether it's an action I failed to do or a harsh word I spoke earlier on, it all tends to surface when I'm alone with my thoughts.

When it comes to my actions or the lack thereof as a mom, I'm usually burdened to the point of shame. Usually it's because of my lack of patience toward my children. Other times it's the moments when I fail to prioritize quality time with my kids.

No matter the weight of regret, I'm always left with a choice. I can either fumble in a pit of despair or look to Christ and respond with a repentant heart.

As God's dearly beloved, we are redeemed by our merciful heavenly Father. He has forgiven our sins and removed our shame so we may live to glorify him. Today we will meditate on his merciful character as we study about his Hebrew name, Elohim Chaseddi, which means "God of Mercy."

TODAY'S PASSAGE: JOEL 2:18–27

Joel is a prophetic book named after its author. The original audience was the people of Judah, the Israelites who broke away from the united kingdom of Israel. Many scholars believe the book of Joel was written during a time of national calamity after the Babylonian exile.

Prior to Joel 2, the author describes the horrendous time and tells the people to lament and return to the Lord. Joel 2:18 is the point in the book where the focus shifts to the Lord's merciful response toward his people.

INTRODUCTION

God's mercy is a display of his goodness. It's essential we understand his mercy is not dependent on anyone. God is merciful because he is good, and he shows mercy to whom he chooses (Exodus 33:19). Let's now begin to unfold the passage together.

The people of Judah were living in a time of turmoil. We can only imagine the amount of suffering they endured. It's important we also understand that in God's good sovereignty, he allowed this destruction on his people (Joel 1:4; 2:25). It was all a part of his righteous judgment because of their unfaithfulness.

In Joel 1 and 2, there is a warning of further judgment on the people (1:15; 2:1) and a call for the people to repent (2:12). Afterward, God promises an outpouring of his mercy. Joel 2:18 is a pivotal point in this passage.

—EXAMINE THE PASSAGE—
WHO IS GOD AND *HOW* IS HE LEADING?

Notice the word *jealous* in Joel 2:18. As you may recall from a previous day from our study, God is jealous for his own honor, and he deserves all the honor because he is holy.

According to this verse, what is the Lord's response to the people?

The word *pity* comes from the Hebrew word *ḥāmal* which translates "to spare, pity, have compassion on."[16] What can you conclude about God's character based on his response toward his people?

Now let's focus on the Lord's promise. Slowly reread the entire passage once more and describe all the things the Lord promises to his people.

As an outpouring of his mercy, God promises blessing after blessing, including restoration. Even when God's people have demonstrated continual unfaithfulness toward him, he is merciful. The promised restoration for God's people would begin with the first coming of Jesus and will be completed with the creation of the new heaven and earth (Romans 8:19–23; Revelation 21:9–27).

As present-day Christians, we live in the "already but not yet" time period. Christ has come to bring us salvation, and now we are awaiting complete restoration, which will be obtained when we are in glory with him. Take a moment to reflect on the many ways God has shown you mercy through his salvation.

Write some of your reflections below.

Consider your role as a mother and how Elohim Chaseddi calls you to lovingly raise your child(ren) in his ways. Give some examples of how you can be merciful toward them (Luke 6:36).

When are you often tempted to harshly respond to your child(ren), and what can you do to be more intentional to respond in a God-honoring way?

When we choose to respond to our children in a way that honors the Lord, we are worshipping him. It also paves the path for us to share the gospel with our children.

Let's now turn our attention toward verses 26 and 27.

What should result from God's merciful response toward his people?

One result is that God's people would never again be put to shame. What a glorious foreshadowing of the gospel! Take a moment to reflect on the ways the Israelites experienced shame as a direct result of their unfaithfulness toward the Lord. (Read Joel 1–2 to gain a better idea of some of the hardship they experienced.)

Now consider how Elohim Chaseddi removes our shame of sin. Romans 8:1 reminds us, "There is therefore now no condemnation for those who are in Christ Jesus." We can live in the freedom of the gospel because of what Christ has done for us. Remembering the truths of the gospel helps us to live in this freedom.

Describe some ways a mom may experience shame.

In what ways does shame hinder our fruitfulness for God's kingdom, including the ministry we have in raising our children?

Look back at the Romans 8:1 mentioned above and write the verse below. As you write it out, prayerfully ask the Lord to sink the truth of his Word deep into your mind and heart.

—ELOHIM CHASEDDI—
OUR MERCIFUL SHEPHERD

Elohim Chaseddi redeemed us from a life of despair and hopelessness. When we are burdened with the shame of our failures as moms, we can look to him with assurance and in repentance. We are recipients of his mercy, and as his dearly beloved, he will lead us to show mercy toward others.

WEEK 3
GROUP DISCUSSION QUESTIONS

INTRODUCTORY QUESTIONS

1. What name of God resonated with you the most this week and why?

2. What is something new you learned this week from your time of study?

DAY 1 — SHOPHET: "JUDGE"

1. Read Psalm 94:1–15. What do you learn about God's character from this passage?

2. Read 2 Corinthians 5:9–10 and Galatians 5:22–23. As you consider your natural tendencies and the temptations you face as a mom, which one specific area do you see the need to grow in during this season of your life?

DAY 2 — ELOHIM: "GOD, MIGHTY CREATOR"

1. Read Genesis 1:26–31. Name some mundane tasks that are reflections of God's creative and orderly character. How can these tasks become a means of worship to God?

2. How can you be more intentional in fulfilling one of God's purposes in your life to "be fruitful and multiply"?

DAY 3 — YAHWEH TSEBAOTH: "THE LORD OF HOSTS"

1. Read 2 Kings 6:8–17. What aspects of motherhood overwhelm you to the point of anxiety or dread, and what are some spiritual benefits to turning to God first?

2. How does the knowledge of who God is—the Lord of hosts—increase your confidence and hope to battle sin?

DAY 4 — *EL EMUNAH*: "THE FAITHFUL GOD"

1.   Read Exodus 6:1–8. Scripture proves God's faithfulness to his people. As you consider the challenges you are facing today, which promise in Scripture will you cling to?

2.   What specific truths will you choose to remember about God's faithfulness when you are faced with discouragement?

DAY 5 — *ELOHIM CHASEDDI*: "GOD OF MERCY"

1.   Read Joel 2:18–27. How can you reflect God's merciful character during interactions with your child(ren)?

2.   Read Romans 8:1. In what ways does shame hinder our fruitfulness for God's kingdom, including the ministry we have in raising our children?

NOTES

Week 4

Miqweh Yisrael

"Hope of Israel"

I'm always hopeful for a better tomorrow when my day doesn't go well. Like on the days when I lack patience with my kids and say words I regret, or on other days when my plans fall by the wayside with messes and sibling squabbles. In moments like these, I hope for a better future, one that is seemingly easier than the current state I'm in.

The problem is, my hope is reliant on my ever-changing circumstances. I'm bound to be disappointed because even ideal circumstances are short-lived.

However, God is unchanging, and we can fully set our hope on him. He is Miqweh Yisrael, which means "Hope of Israel." He is the one who saves those who put their trust in him.[17] Today we will discover more of him and be encouraged to put our hope in him when daily challenges cause us to despair.

Today's Passage: Ezekiel 36:22–28

We will begin our time of study in the book of Ezekiel, which was written by the prophet Ezekiel. Its purpose was to proclaim a time of judgment and restoration to the exiled Jews, who were living in Babylon at the time. Chapter 36 contains a prophecy of restoration for God's people.

INTRODUCTION

Shortly before Ezekiel 36:18, the prophet Ezekiel wrote about how God poured out his wrath on his people because of their unfaithfulness. Now we read about God's plan for restoration, which began with the coming of Jesus Christ and will reach its fulfillment with the new heaven and earth.

In this passage, there is a contrast between the holiness of God and the sinfulness of the people. What was the sin committed by the people?

—EXAMINE THE PASSAGE—
WHO IS GOD AND *HOW* IS HE LEADING?

According to Ezekiel 36:22–23, why was God going to restore his people?

As we learned earlier, God is holy, and only he is deserving of honor and glory because he is the standard for righteousness. Anyone or anything else is undeserving. In righteous justice, God poured out his wrath on his people. Then, he promised restoration. God's plan for restoration is further proof of his holiness because his actions are purely good.

When Ezekiel wrote this passage, God's people were in exile and scattered. According to verse 24, what would initiate their restoration?

Summarize how God would restore his people according to Ezekiel 36:25–27.

Verse 27 contains the promise of the Holy Spirit, which his people later received after the ascension of Jesus (Acts 1:1–8; 2:1–13). According to Ezekiel 36:27, what would the Spirit enable God's people to do?

Try and imagine the original audience of Ezekiel 36, scattered and living in exile. They were the scorn of many nations and the recipients of God's wrath. Now God was promising them restoration for the sake of his holy name. While they continued to live out their time in exile, they had this promise of redemption from the author of hope, Miqweh Yisrael.

Like the Israelites who were exiled in Babylon, we are also living out a time of exile here on earth, since heaven is our home. Inevitably, living as exiles in a "foreign land" causes lots of strife for us.

Take a moment to pinpoint specific challenges related to motherhood that result in feelings of hopelessness.

When you are burdened with the challenges of motherhood, what tends to fuel your hope (e.g., the next best thing, more time to yourself, the next stage of child-rearing, more money to buy items of comfort, etc.)?

Let's now turn to Hebrews, where the author writes about the certainty of God's promise of salvation. Please read Hebrews 6:19–20.

Through Jesus' work, we live in the partial reality of the hope of restoration that was promised in Ezekiel 36; however, our redemption is not yet fully realized. It will reach its fulfillment with the creation of the new heaven and earth (Romans 8:19–23; Revelation 21:9–27).

Describe the hope that we have in Jesus according to Hebrews 6:19–20.

Instead of other people and things of this world, the anchor for our soul is the hope we have in Miqweh Yisrael. Nothing else will do. It's the hope that fuels our joy, knowing that he is conforming us into a pure bride of heaven, where one day our restoration *will* be complete in glory.

How does a gospel-centered hope impact the feelings of hopelessness we might experience while navigating challenging days or seasons of motherhood?

Name some practical ways you can keep a gospel-centered hope at the forefront of your mind during the week.

Real hope is the source of true joy. Knowing it should compel us to share it with others. Think about the moments of disappointment your children might experience as they grow up.

What are some practical ways you can direct them to lasting hope?

Consider your sphere of influence and the other people with whom you may come in contact with, both Christians and non-Christians.

What are some ways you can share the joy of Miqweh Yisrael with them?

—*MIQWEH YISRAEL*—
OUR SHEPHERD WHO IS OUR HOPE

Miqweh Yisrael is the sure and steady anchor for our souls. As we live out our time of exile here on earth, we must continually set our hope on him. Whether we are completing mundane tasks or persevering through a difficult trial, Miqweh Yisrael will fill us with eternal joy. Our hope is found in him.

El Olam

"The Everlasting God"

Watching my daughters grow over the years is a subtle yet constant reminder that they will one day be on their own. Gone are the simple days when they were swaddled and resting securely in my arms. Scraped knees and hurt feelings are now a part of their ever-changing life. And I'm stuck in the tension of wanting to always be there for them and recognizing the need to let go.

While my heart aches knowing my children are growing in their independence, I also trust in God's ever-present character. Even though I can't always be with my children, God is with them. I can entrust them into his care.

Our loving heavenly Father is omnipresent, omnipotent, and omniscient. He is El Olam, which means "The Everlasting God." Today we will learn more about and develop our trust in his eternal character.

Today's Passage: Psalm 90:1–6

As you may recall, the book of Psalms is a compilation of poetry and contains a lot of figurative language. Psalm 90 in particular is a psalm of lament written by Moses. There is a contrast in the psalm between the shortness of man's life and God's eternal existence.

INTRODUCTION

God is not a created being. He has always existed, and he will always exist. Revelation 1:8 says, "'I am the Alpha and the Omega,' says the Lord God, 'who is and who was and who is to come, the Almighty.'" Even though the concept of God's existence is something we will never fully comprehend, developing our understanding will enable us to better understand his character and ways. It will also deepen our trust in all the promises he has made.

—EXAMINE THE PASSAGE—
WHO IS GOD AND *HOW* IS HE LEADING?

What does verse 2 reveal about El Olam?

What is the psalmist poetically communicating about God's concept of time in verses 4–6?

How does the knowledge of God's concept of time affect your perspective on current circumstances?

Since God is without a beginning or an end, this also signifies that his ways are everlasting. Consider all the names of God we have studied up until this point. Briefly list some of his attributes.

We can depend on El Olam to be the same today and forever (Hebrews 13:8). All of who he is will remain, even when we are no longer here on earth. Undoubtedly, God is our dwelling place year after year. He is enduring, and we will always be secure in him.

Think about all the daily tasks you complete each day for your family. How does confidence in God's enduring character strengthen your desire to faithfully honor him?

Describe how a steadfast faith in El Olam increases your trust for him to care for your child(ren) (Isaiah 40:11).

El Olam's promises are everlasting, which means we can fully rely on the promises he made in Scripture thousands of years ago. We can also expect them to endure through eternity. Isaiah 40:7–8 says, "The grass withers, the flower fades when the breath of the LORD blows on it; surely the people are grass. The grass withers, the flower fades, but the word of our God will stand forever." All of God's Word will endure forever.

Take a moment to reference a few promises in Scripture.

Most importantly, our salvation is secure in El Olam. Let's now turn our attention to Hebrews, where the author focused on Christ as the greater mediator of a new covenant. Please read Hebrews 9:11–15.

Notice the word *eternal* every time it appears in Hebrews 9:11–15. Now complete the following statements

We have an eternal _____ (9:12)

Jesus Christ offered his blood for the redemption of our sin through the eternal _____ (9:14)

Recipients of the new covenant will receive an eternal _____ (9:15).

No matter our current circumstances, our present sin, or whatever may lie ahead in the future, our redemption through Jesus is secure. It's eternal. We always have a reason to rejoice! Our hope remains steadfast in El Olam.

How might these truths impact you when you struggle to move past "mom guilt"?

—*EL OLAM*—

OUR EVERLASTING SHEPHERD

El Olam is constant, boundless, timeless, and unceasing. Other people and things will eventually fade away, but God will eternally remain. We can entrust our children into his care, receive help from his enduring character, rest in his unending promises, and rejoice in our secure future with him. From everlasting to everlasting, he is God.

DAY 3

El Elyon

"God Most High"

Motherhood is full of unexpected challenges. No matter how prepared we may feel at times, there are some things we can never prepare for. Like the times when a teething baby keeps us up at night, a child's illness brings us to our knees, or a teenager's decision weighs heavily on our hearts.

Despite the challenges, we can rest secure in the sovereignty of God. In ways we will never fathom, he is able to use these challenges to develop our character, strengthen our trust in him, and prepare us for later trials. We can be encouraged in knowing that everything is perfectly orchestrated and ordained by him.

He is El Elyon, which means "God Most High." His character is matchless, and he reigns supreme. Today we will learn more about him and develop our trust in him when he allows unexpected challenges in our life.

Today's Passage: Job 1:6–22

As you may recall from a previous day of study, the book of Job recounts the life of a faithful man of God who experienced great suffering. In chapter 1, we learn about how all the trials in Job's life began.

INTRODUCTION

The spiritual realm is such a mystery, but we obtain a glimpse of it in this passage of Scripture. Undoubtedly, this is also a passage that raises many questions like, "Why did God allow this to happen?" and "Does God cause evil?" The sovereignty of El Elyon is certainly a complex attribute of God, one that we will never fully understand and one in which we must be careful not to misinterpret.

Let's begin to study this passage together and make conclusions of El Elyon based on what Scripture reveals.

—EXAMINE THE PASSAGE—
WHO IS GOD AND *HOW* IS HE LEADING?

According to Job 1:9–10, what started all the calamity in Job's life? Describe the rationale that was presented to God.

What does verse 12 reveal about El Elyon?

God is the supreme ruler over every realm. Nothing happens without his authority. In your own words, briefly summarize all that occurred after the Lord allowed Satan to afflict Job.

It's essential for us to understand that "Scripture nowhere shows God as directly doing anything evil, but rather as bringing about evil deeds through the willing actions of moral creatures."[18] Several examples in Scripture convey this truth (e.g., Genesis 37; 45:5; 50:20; Exodus 14:4).

For the past several weeks, we have studied the names of God and the attributes from which the names are derived. All these characteristics of God are true, and all of them must be upheld as a whole. As we develop our understanding of El Elyon, we must remember that in his sovereignty, he is fully merciful, faithful, righteous, and just.

God sovereignly allowed Satan to have his way with Job, which allowed God to shepherd Job in a way that revealed responses of his heart that would not otherwise be visible. Let's now look together at verses 20–21.

Describe both Job's response to his adversity and his trust in God.

Job knew God was the one who allowed the hardship in his life, yet he never blamed God for evil. What does verse 22 reveal about Job's response?

As present-day readers of the Bible, we have the wide-angle perspective of this passage. We know how the spiritual realm was involved, and we can read about how the story unfolds. Job's perspective was different. He was a man of God who experienced unfathomable hardship, but despite it all, he chose to worship God.

How does worshipping God amid the challenges of motherhood change our outlook and develop our trust in El Elyon?

Life is full of challenges, some of which are caused by our own sin. Other times, God simply allows hardship in our lives for purposes we may never comprehend (Isaiah 55:8).

Describe the difference between a mom who has a self-centered perspective of unwelcomed hardship and one whose unwavering faith trusts in our good, sovereign God.

How can you guard yourself from doubting El Elyon's character when he allows hardship in your life?

All that the Lord allows in our lives is purposed for good, even when we don't understand his ways. In fact, Romans 8:28 tells us, "And we know that for those who love God all things work together for good, for those who are called according to his purpose."

Recall a time in your life when God used hardship for your good.

—EL ELYON—

OUR SOVEREIGN SHEPHERD

El Elyon is perfect in all his ways and loving to all he has made. Today you may groan in frustration in response to your motherhood woes, but God may be developing your perseverance, sanctifying you for good works, or growing your reliance on him. Whatever challenge you face today, be encouraged in knowing that none of it is orchestrated in vain. God knows you and loves you. His power and authority are supreme, and you can trust his good plans.

Yahweh Nissi

"The Lord My Banner"

Many years ago, one of my daughters went through a challenging stage. Unfortunately, it wasn't short-lived, and I struggled with patience on a daily basis. One day, in my weary state, I managed to write out a specific prayer to the Lord. Thankfully, the written prayer not only helped me to ask for specific requests related to my circumstances but also helped me to continually seek God when my heart grew apathetic.

Inevitably, this prayer became a means for me to continually proclaim, "God is with me, and he will give me what I need to help me through this."

The Israelites did something similar to proclaim their steadfast faith in God during times of warfare, except their proclamation was a banner. When they claimed victory over their first battle after leaving Egypt, Moses made an altar and named it Yahweh Nissi, which means "The Lord My Banner."

Today we will learn more about this unique name of God and develop our understanding of what it signifies.

Today's Passage: Exodus 17:8–16

Shortly before Exodus 17:8–16, the Israelites crossed the Red Sea after leaving Egypt. They were now journeying through a wilderness, depending on God's daily provision, when the Amalekites attacked them.

INTRODUCTION

Imagine how weary the Israelites must have felt after escaping the threat of the Egyptians and traveling through the wilderness. Then the Amalekites attacked. It was the Israelites' first battle on their journey to eventually conquer the Promised Land. Despite their circumstances, they displayed an unwavering faith in Yahweh Nissi.

—EXAMINE THE PASSAGE—
WHO IS GOD AND *HOW* IS HE LEADING?

The staff Moses held in his hand was no ordinary wooden stick. It was the same staff that he used to display God's mighty power during the plagues of Egypt (Exodus 4:17), in the crossing of the Red Sea (Exodus 14:16), and through the provision of water from a rock (Exodus 17:5–7).

The staff Moses held in his hand was a symbol or banner of God's power. It was a proclamation of their continued trust in the Lord who delivered them out of Egypt.

According to verses 10–11, describe what Moses was doing with the staff.

Consider the significance of the staff up until this point in the history of Israel. What did the staff signify for the Israelites during this first battle?

In many ways, the Israelites' deliverance from Egypt was foreshadowing what God would eventually do for his people in providing deliverance through Jesus. In fact, we can relate to a lot of the Israelites' journey from Egypt to the Promised Land. Like the Israelites, God delivered us from a bondage (of sin). We, too, are journeying through our time here on earth until we reach the "Promised Land" of heaven (Romans 8:18–21). And just like the Israelites fought their enemies on their journey to the Promised Land, we will also have to fight battles, including the ones against our sinful flesh, the darkness of this world, and demonic forces (Ephesians 6:12).

Take a moment to write down some temptations you are battling right now.

When we turn to Yahweh Nissi amid trials and temptations, we are turning to the one who has the power to help us overcome (Galatians 5:24–25; 2 Corinthians 10:3–5).[19] The Lord is our banner, just like he was for the Israelites.

What are some gospel truths you can keep at the forefront of your mind when you are faced with trials and temptations? If you need some help, the following verses contain excellent gospel truths: Romans 6:12–14; 8:1, 10–11, 31, 37–39.

Before we conclude our study, let's go back to Exodus 17:12–13 and discuss these verses together. Describe the significance of what Aaron and Hur did for Moses.

Think of other moms within your sphere of influence. In what ways can you also serve your sisters in Christ by pointing them to Yahweh Nissi when they are going through unexpected motherhood challenges?

—*YAHWEH NISSI*—

OUR SHEPHERD WHO IS OUR BANNER

Yahweh Nissi gave us the victory of salvation through the death of his Son. Through him, we have the power to overcome any foe (1 John 5:4–5). When we face daily trials and temptations in motherhood, we can turn to him for the guidance, strength, and perseverance we need.

DAY 5

Yahweh

"Lord"

As a new mom, I wandered in a spiritual desert for a long time. I wandered because I often neglected time with the Lord. I kept waiting for life to settle down so I could be better rested and less distracted as I opened God's Word, but these ideal moments rarely came. Instead, when the challenges of life overwhelmed me, I turned to temporary comforts. Rather than primarily seeking the Lord for guidance, I turned to insufficient means of help.

My daughter was almost a year old when I finally began pursuing the Lord with whatever time and energy I had. I learned to seek him in the quiet and in the chaos, in the morning and throughout my day. Even though the challenges of motherhood remained, my hope was renewed as I consistently abided in the Lord, my Shepherd.

Whatever stage of parenting we may be in, whether it's raising infants or teenagers, we will always be faced with a choice. Will we attempt to navigate motherhood alone, or will we continually turn to the Lord, our all-sufficient Shepherd who promises to gently lead us?

Today we will learn more about Yahweh, which is translated "Lord." Out of all the Hebrew names of God we have studied, it is the only name given by God himself. It is the personal and divine name for God, which is associated with the redemptive acts for his people.[20]

Today's Passage: Exodus 3

As you may recall from a previous day of study, the book of Exodus recounts the Israelites' deliverance from the Egyptians. Prior to Exodus 3, God raised up Moses, who would eventually be the one to lead the Israelites out of Egypt. Remarkably, Moses grew up as a son to Pharaoh's daughter, even though he was an Israelite; however, he later fled from Pharaoh after murdering an Egyptian. In chapter 3, he was living in Midian with his family.

INTRODUCTION

Moses was in an ordinary place when the angel of the Lord appeared to him in an extraordinary way. Some scholars have concluded the angel of the Lord to be God himself.[21] One reason is because the flame of fire signified God's presence in other passages of Scripture (Exodus 13:21–22; 19:18; 40:38). Also, the angel of the Lord is directly identified as "the LORD" and "God" in Exodus 3:4.

—EXAMINE THE PASSAGE—
WHO IS GOD AND HOW IS HE LEADING?

In your own words, summarize the Lord's message to Moses in Exodus 3:7–10.

Each time we study Scripture, it's important for us to consider what the specific passage reveals about God's character because it allows us to deepen our understanding of who he is. Consider what the Lord told Moses in Exodus 3:7–10.

What do these verses reveal about God's character?

In verse 11, Moses doubted his ability to complete the task the Lord called him to do. What was the Lord's response to Moses?

Sometimes we also doubt our ability to fulfill a specific task the Lord has called us to do. Consider the moments of discouragement you have experienced in the past related to your ability to parent your child(ren).

Name some reasons for the discouragement.

We are God's workmanship, created to do good works (Ephesians 2:10). Even though the task of raising our children is very different from the task Moses had, the promise of God's presence is the same. In fact, God promises his people numerous times in Scripture that he will be with them.

In what way should the promise of God's presence affect our struggle with discouragement?

God had a plan to deliver the Israelites from slavery just like he had a plan to deliver us through the death of his Son. In Exodus 3:14–15, God reveals his name to Moses, the name that from then on would always be associated with the redemption of his chosen people.[22]

Before God revealed his name as Yahweh in verse 15, he told Moses, "I AM WHO I AM" (Exodus 3:14). The statement God made about himself provided a description of his character. Because the "I AM" statement is connected to the revealed name of God as Yahweh, we can conclude that Yahweh signifies

God's eternal existence, absolute independence, and constant nature. He is also the most valuable and absolute reality who is the standard of truth, and everything is dependent on him.[23]

Such a description is marvelously profound. Take a moment to reflect on who Yahweh is. Write some of your reflections in the space provided.

If we were to read further on in Exodus, we would see how Yahweh was with Moses and how he equipped him for the specific task of leading his people out of Egypt.

In what ways does the truth of Yahweh's character strengthen your trust in his ability to lead you as you fulfill your role as a mom?

Let's now turn our attention to the New Testament, where John the apostle writes about Jesus' interaction with the Jews while he was teaching in the temple. In this passage, we will see how the Jews rejected Jesus' revelation in saying he is God. Please read John 8:48–59.

What statement did Jesus make about himself in verse 58?

Only God is transcendent over time, and Jesus is attributing this characteristic to himself when he said, "I am." By claiming his divinity, Jesus is also saying that he is the same God who appeared to Moses in the burning bush.

The same God who delivered the Israelites out of Egypt is the same one who came down in human form to deliver his people from sin through his death and resurrection. Yahweh's character proved true for the Israelites, and it does for us as well. He is the covenant keeping God who redeemed us from a life of despair. We can trust him.

Consider all of who you are as a woman of God and the specific tasks you accomplish each day as a mom. Try and pinpoint one of the main reasons why you may often or occasionally struggle to seek Yahweh and continually abide in him each day.

When motherhood challenges arise, it may be easier for us to escape via a quick scroll on our phones, seek temporary comforts, or find answers to our most pressing questions via an online search engine. All of these earthly things have a place in our lives, but we shouldn't use them as a substitute for Yahweh, our all-sufficient Shepherd.

What are some of the things you tend to do first when parenting challenges arise?

What can you do the next time you are tempted to find security and help in other people or things more than Yahweh? Take your time to consider how you can practically put off your old ways and replace them with God-honoring habits (Ephesians 4:20–24).

As we conclude our Bible study, what are some specific truths you want to keep at the forefront of your mind from this day forward?

—*YAHWEH*—

OUR SHEPHERD WHO IS LORD

Yahweh is and will always be. Whether we're sleep-deprived with an infant in tow, raising school-aged kids, or navigating our child's teenage years, we can trust him to lead us. Yahweh is our all-sufficient Shepherd, the one who graciously redeemed us, and the one who promises to gently lead us.

"He will tend his flock like a shepherd; he will gather the lambs in his arms;
he will carry them in his bosom, and gently lead those that are with young."

—Isaiah 40:11

WEEK 4
GROUP DISCUSSION QUESTIONS

INTRODUCTORY QUESTIONS

1. What name of God resonated with you the most this week and why?

2. What is something new you learned this week from your time of study?

DAY 1 — *MIQWEH YISRAEL*: "HOPE OF ISRAEL"

1. Read Ezekiel 36:22–28. Describe how God would restore his people according to this passage.

2. Read Hebrews 6:19–20. How does a gospel-centered hope impact the feelings of hopelessness you might experience while navigating challenging days of motherhood?

DAY 2 — *EL OLAM*: "THE EVERLASTING GOD"

1. Read Psalm 90:1–6. How does the knowledge of God's concept of time impact your perspective on current circumstances?

2. Describe how a steadfast faith in El Olam increases your trust for him to care for your child(ren) (Isaiah 40:11).

DAY 3 — *EL ELYON*: "GOD MOST HIGH"

1. Read Job 1:6–22. What does this passage reveal about the sovereignty of God?

2. Read Romans 8:28. Describe the difference between a mom who has a self-centered perspective of unwelcomed hardship and one whose unwavering faith trusts in our good, sovereign God.

DAY 4 — *YAHWEH NISSI*: "THE LORD MY BANNER"

1. Read Exodus 17:8–16. Revisit this day's study and describe the significance of the staff held by Moses during the battle.

2. In what ways can you serve your sisters in Christ by pointing them to Yahweh Nissi when they are going through unexpected motherhood challenges?

DAY 5 — *YAHWEH*: "LORD"

1. Read Exodus 3:13–14. In what ways does the truth of Yahweh's character strengthen your trust in his ability to lead you as you fulfill your role as a mom?

2. What are some specific truths you want to keep at the forefront of your mind from this day forward?

NOTES

FINAL WORD

As we come to the end of our time together, I pray the Spirit has led you into a time of refreshment and that you are overflowing with hope and trust for our all-sufficient Shepherd.

What you choose to do from this day forward is up to you. As we all know, motherhood is busy. Quiet moments with the Lord require intentionality. They require a plan. Now that we know God is our all-sufficient Shepherd who promises to gently lead us, how will we continue to seek him from this day forward?

Some days it will be harder than others, and there will be moments when scrolling through our phone for visual comfort will be easier than taking a minute to share our frustrations with our Lord. How can we seek the Lord's guidance more often? We can do this with small, consistent steps forward and through the help of the Holy Spirit working within us.

As a fellow sister in Christ and as a well-seasoned mom, I'd like to offer a few suggestions for how you can continue to spend time with the Lord with whatever time you may have on hand:

1. Listen to Scripture on a Bible app.

2. Place one verse on a card and put it where you'll see it often.

3. Start with a five- to ten-minute commitment of reading your Bible each day.

4. Read one verse in Proverbs and meditate on it throughout your day.

5. Place your open Bible somewhere you might see it often.

6. Set aside a specific time during the day to commit to time with God.

7. Pull up your Bible app to read while waiting in a check-out line or during your lunch break.

However you decide to spend time with the Lord, I pray you will continue to grow in the knowledge of who God is so that you may continuously overflow with hope and trust in him.

NOTES

1 *ESV Study Bible*, (Wheaton, IL: Crossway Books, 2008).

2 "rāʿâ," Strong's Hebrew Lexicon (ESV), H7462, https://www.blueletterbible.org//lang/lexicon/lexicon.cfm?Strongs=H7462&t=ESV.

3 "qāḇaṣ," Strong's Hebrew Lexicon (ESV), H6908, https://www.blueletterbible.org//lang/lexicon/lexicon.cfm?Strongs=H6908&t=ESV.

4 "nāśāʾ," Strong's Hebrew Lexicon (ESV), H5375, https://www.blueletterbible.org//lang/lexicon/lexicon.cfm?Strongs=H5375&t=ESV.

5 "nāhal," Strong's Hebrew Lexicon (ESV), H5095, https://www.blueletterbible.org//lang/lexicon/lexicon.cfm?Strongs=H5095&t=ESV.

6 Bible Gateway, s.v. "rock," https://www.biblegateway.com/resources/dictionary-of-bible-themes/4354-rock, accessed January 5, 2021.

7 Currid, J., et al. Study Notes on Leviticus, *The ESV Study Bible* (Wheaton, IL: Crossway 2008), 217.

8 "Yᵊhōvâ yirʾê," Strong's Hebrew Lexicon (ESV), H3070, https://www.blueletterbible.org//lang/lexicon/lexicon.cfm?Strongs=H3070&t=ESV.

9 John Piper, "My Name is God Almighty", September 30, 1984, https://www.desiringgod.org/messages/my-name-is-god-almighty

10 "qāvâ," Strong's Hebrew Lexicon (ESV), H6960, https://www.blueletterbible.org//lang/lexicon/lexicon.cfm?Strongs=H6960&t=ESV.

11 Wayne Grudem, *Systematic Theology* (Grand Rapids: Zondervan, 1994), 202.

12 Grudem, *Systematic Theology*, 205.

13 "yārēʾ," Strong's Hebrew Lexicon (ESV), H3372, https://www.blueletterbible.org//lang/lexicon/lexicon.cfm?Strongs=H3372&t=ESV.

14 Alexander, D. Study Notes on Genesis, *The ESV Study Bible* (Wheaton, IL: Crossway 2008), 51.

15 "šānan," Strong's Hebrew Lexicon (ESV), H8150, https://www.blueletterbible.org//lang/lexicon/lexicon.cfm?Strongs=H8150&t=ESV.

16 "ḥāmal," Strong's Hebrew Lexicon (ESV), H2550, https://www.blueletterbible.org//lang/lexicon/lexicon.cfm?Strongs=H2550&t=ESV.

17 Ann Spangler, *The Names of God: 52 Bible Studies for Individuals and Groups* (Grand Rapids, MI: Zondervan, 2009), 106.

18 Grudem, *Systematic Theology*, 323.

19 Ann Spangler, *Praying the Names of God* (Grand Rapids, MI: Zondervan, 2004), 109.

20 Spangler, *Praying the Names of God*, 74.

21 Harris, K., Study Notes on Exodus, *The ESV Study Bible* (Wheaton, IL: Crossway 2008) 148.

22 Spangler, *Praying the Names of God*, 80.

23 Piper, "Ten Things 'Yahweh' Means," Desiring God, August 5, 2012, https://www.desiringgod.org/articles/10-things-yahweh-means.

Acknowledgments

First and foremost, I thank Jesus Christ, my Savior. You are everything to me, Lord. It is a privilege to be able to proclaim your all-sufficiency to the world. Thank you for equipping me with everything I needed to fulfill this very specific purpose for your glory. I would write another book all over again if it means I get to journey together with you in your Word as I write.

To my husband, Adam: thank you for encouraging me to pursue this big dream of mine years ago when it all began as a small idea in conversation with you. Countless times you've given up hours in your day to watch our girls in order to give me a few hours to study and write in a quiet house. Thank you, love. You have been my biggest support, aside from our Lord. Without you, I'm not sure I would have had the courage to write this book.

To my daughters, Tahlia, Elyza, and Lydia: all of you are a precious gift to me. Life is so joyfully full because of you all. Thank you for supporting me with sweet notes, wildflowers, and chocolate chips while I spent countless hours writing this book. I pray these words I've written will fuel your hope one day, as you grow in the knowledge of who God is.

To my dad and mom, Tom and Consuelo Burgess: Dad, I wish you could be with me today, but I know our good Lord had other plans. This book is written in memory of you. Mom, thank you for always supporting me in whatever dream I ever had. You've said yes to so many of my wild ideas throughout my lifetime, and I know I would not have had the audacity to pursue them if it were not for your constant encouragement for me to do so. Most importantly, thank you Dad and Mom for teaching me the ways of the Lord at an early age. I'm eternally grateful that you both faithfully kept pointing me to Jesus since I was a young girl.

To my brother, Stephen: thank you for cheering me on throughout the past few years and offering words of encouragement to me on countless occasions.

To my in-laws, Doug and Nancy Bretschneider: thank you for praying for me, offering words of wisdom when I needed it, and supporting me with verses of encouragement throughout the process of writing this book. Your lives are a beautiful reflection of Christ. I owe a lot of my spiritual growth to you both, and I'm thankful to have you as my second parents.

To my pastors, Jon Mark Olesky and Kent Langham: thank you for faithfully upholding the Word in your sermons each week. I know my passion for Bible literacy is a direct result of being a part of our church, which is largely a result of your leadership. Thank you both for taking the time to review my unpolished manuscript and offering feedback on the theological content.

To Andrea Housam, Hannah Williamson, Kristin Hargett, Molly Langham, Rebekah Almond, and Stacy Bentley: thank you for taking the time to review my first sample manuscript. The suggestions you gave me in the very beginning enabled me to make necessary improvements to this Bible study.

To my beta readers, Christin Szczesniak, Jennifer Pearson, and Kelly Bestgen: thank you for investing your time into this book. The hours you put into reading the manuscript and offering feedback were not in vain.

To Michelle Bretschneider, Stacy Bentley, and Kelly Griffin: all three of you have been my biggest cheerleaders since I shared my idea of writing a book with you all years ago. Thanks for sharing my excitement as I pursued this dream of mine and for encouraging me right from the start. Your zeal for the Lord and his work was always very apparent.

To Sarah Koontz: God has used you as a ministry mentor in my life, and I'm so grateful for all the wisdom I've gleaned while working with you. Thank you for offering words of advice and guidance when I first told you about this book.

To all the ladies at my church (you know who you are): thank you for offering words of encouragement and prayers for me over the past few years when this whole book journey began as a blog.

To the team invested in the publication of this book, Rachel Adamus, Melinda Martin, Whitney Bak, Andrew Buss, Sarah Geringer, and Julianna Steen: thank you for contributing countless hours to the publication of this book. You are the team who has taken my words and ideas and brought this book to life.

ABOUT THE AUTHOR
SANDRA BRETSCHNEIDER

SANDRA BRETSCHNEIDER is a wife, mother of three, speech-language pathologist, and writer with a passion to help other women to dive deeper into God's Word. Her interest in Bible literacy led her to pursue a certificate in biblical studies, which has equipped her to author several Bible studies for her online ministry as well as write supplemental Bible-study content as a creative partner for Living by Design Ministries. She and her family reside in Florida with their energetic goldendoodle.

If you enjoyed this Bible study,
please consider leaving an online review
on Amazon, Goodreads, or Barnes & Noble.

Made in the USA
Monee, IL
05 April 2023

31379729R10083